DISCARD

NATURE PROJECTS FOR YOUNG SCIENTISTS

Revised Edition

Kenneth G. Rainis

FRANKLIN WATTS
A Division of Scholastic Inc.
New York ▪ Toronto ▪ London ▪ Auckland ▪ Sydney ▪
Mexico City ▪ New Delhi ▪ Hong Kong
Danbury, Connecticut

First Edition

In memory of my father,
Vincent Rainis, my best friend
and a lover of books.

Second Edition

For my daughter, Caroline—
who adds sparkle to her mother's
and my lives!

Photographs © 2002: Bruce J. Russell/BioMEDIA Associates: cover, 50, 62 bottom, 62 center, 62 top, 66 bottom left, 66 bottom right, 66 center left, 66 top right, 66 top left; Gervase Pevarnik: 71, 72, 72 top; Kenneth G. Rainis: 176; Neo/SCI Corporation: 63.

NOTE TO READERS:
Throughout this book, most measurements are given only in metric units because that is the system of measure used by most professional scientists.

Library of Congress Cataloging-in-Publication Data

Rainis, Kenneth G.
    Nature projects for young scientists / Kenneth G. Rainis.—2nd ed.
        p. cm.—(Projects for young scientists)
    Rev. ed. of: Nature. 1989.
    Includes bibliographical references (p.).
    ISBN 0-531-11724-3 (lib. bdg.)   0-531-16381-4 (pbk.)
    1. Natural history projects—Juvenile literature. [1. Natural history—Experiments. 2. Experiments.] I. Rainis, Kenneth G. Nature. II. Title. III. Series.
    QH55 .R35 2001
    508'.078—dc21   2001017582

ACKNOWLEDGMENTS

This book would not have become a reality without the loving support of my wife, Joan. Thanks to my partners at Neo/SCI: Kurt Gelke, Jean Coniber, and George Nassis, whose support is greatly appreciated. Special thanks to Ken Rando and Brian Romanko who, as always, helped me with the electrons. Thanks to John Minichiello for counsel on things that "percolate." Many of the photomicrographs in the book were created by my good friend, Bruce Russell, whose technical and aesthetic talents have added a special dimension to this work. Henry Rasof, the first edition editor, was instrumental in getting it all started. This second edition is much the better for the support and critical comment of Melissa Palestro.

C O N T E N T S

CHAPTER EIGHT

CHAPTER 1

BECOMING A NATURE DETECTIVE

Nature can be viewed as a series of solutions to the problems of self-preservation and self-perpetuation. All life on Earth must take in nourishment, adjust to its environment, defend itself against predators, and reproduce. The variety, complexity, and beauty of nature result from each life-form's unique solution to these tasks. The naturalist studies these solutions.

A naturalist often operates as a kind of nature detective. Like scientists and detectives, the naturalist uses the scientific method to probe and understand nature's secrets.

observation → reasoned guess → test → conclusion

As a nature detective, you will work hard to observe what is happening around you, make a reasoned guess (a *hypothesis*) to explain what you observed, design a method (an *experiment*) to test your hypothesis, and use your results (*data*) to conclude whether your thought was correct or whether it should be changed. A good experiment tries to control all of the differences (or *variables*) except the one you are studying, called the *experimental variable*. Sometimes you will need to establish a "normal" or unchanged group (a *control*) against which to compare your results. A *control group* helps you determine whether your experimental results are valid. It will help you link a planned change with an effect in the experimental group—or discover that it produced no effect in comparison with the control.

Like all great naturalists, scientists, and detectives, you will find that your powers of observation will provide the springboard to your investigations. At times, your investigations will be aided by serendipity—the phenomenon of finding something valuable while you are looking for something else. Although everyone has these experiences, they are meaningless unless you can recognize their value. As the great scientist Louis Pasteur said, "Chance favors the prepared mind."

CLASSIFYING LIFE-FORMS

One of the greatest of all naturalists, Carolus Linnaeus (1707-78), originated the concept of classifying living things in an orderly and scientific manner. His major work, *Systema Naturae*, is still used as a foundation for classifying organisms. Scientists continue to identify organisms by a two-part Latin name consisting of the genus and the species. For example, *Acer saccharum* is the scientific name for the sugar maple.

Today, scientists recognize five groups of life, called kingdoms. This five-kingdom scheme includes monerans (bacteria), fungi, protists (algae and protozoa), plants, and animals. The chapters in this book are also divided in this fashion, going from bacteria, the simplest of organisms, to vertebrate animals, the most complex. An excellent guide to the kingdoms of life on Earth is *Five Kingdoms* by Lynn Margulis and Karlene V. Schwartz, which contains valuable information for naturalists at all levels.

THE PROJECTS IN THIS BOOK

The projects in this book are designed to help you learn more about nature and about yourself. Some of the projects are easy; some are difficult. Some are presented in step-by-step fashion, while others are simply ideas for you to develop.

You can work through the projects systematically to learn something about the different life-forms on Earth, or you can choose one project that appeals to you. Either way, you will wind up with an experience that is enriching for its own sake, that may satisfy a class requirement, or that may be suitable for a science fair project.

Since classroom assignments and science fairs require careful methodology and formal presentation, you may need to do a lot of planning before you actually begin a project. You will want to take careful notes as you go along. Take time to obtain and organize background information about a subject you will be investigating. Such information will help you understand the "bigger picture" as well as identify possible experimental variables. Being able to understand an experimental result is as important as producing one.

For a valuable project that does not have to utilize all the steps of the scientific method, you could do a general investigation of microlife in a city pond and accompany your results with photographs of the pond, drawings of the organisms observed, and information about your sampling locations and methods.

On the other hand, suppose you observe that bees are attracted to yellow flowers. You might want to prove that the color yellow attracts bees. You could conduct an experiment to test this hypothesis by preparing two identical paper models—one red, the other yellow. If you observe that a bee lands on the yellow flower, have you proven your hypothesis? No, you have only gathered evidence (data) to support the hypothesis. There may be other variables, like flower shape or odor, that you have not investigated. You must conduct additional experiments that eliminate as many variables as possible before you have enough information to prove the hypothesis.

Both projects are legitimate and scientifically sound, and both have their place, but each will appeal to a different kind of naturalist/scientist. Science is the process of inquiry—one way of gaining knowledge about the world.

INTERNET PROSPECTING

The Internet is a dynamic matrix of interlinked computer networks that is waiting to be explored. Its singular success—its redundancy—is possible because the Internet was originally designed to break a transmitted data stream into discreet "packets" of information. If one "packet" was lost, it could be identified and sent again, even by another route, to its assigned destination. Every website on the Internet has its own unique identification, or address, known as the uniform resource locator, or URL. The URL consists of a string of letters or numbers, such as http://www.enature.com.

In each URL, the letters preceding the colon denote the method used to access portions of the Internet:

http: hypertext transfer protocol—hypertext technology that links all sites (pages) on the World Wide Web, the graphic part of the Internet, by using programs (browsers) to present information to the viewer.

ftp: file transfer protocol—technology that allows a file to be downloaded to your computer.

Telnet: allows logging on to a site's computer to access its database information.

Gopher: an Internet application that catalogs millions of files residing on computers worldwide and makes this information easy to retrieve.

The letters and numbers after the colon, which are always accompanied by a double slash, identify the specific computer site to which you will be connecting—in this case, the World Wide Web. Letters and numbers between periods identify the website. Letters such as com, org, or gov identify the server type—com = commercial; org = organization; gov = government. Additional characters following another backslash denote a specific directory on the serving computer's hard drive.

SURFING THE WEB

The technology of Web browsers (user programs) continues to evolve at a phenomenal pace. Netscape's *Navigator* and Microsoft's *Internet Explorer* are constantly upgrading to provide as dynamic a graphic access to the Web as possible. Multiprotocol browsers, like Netscape, also allow access to Gopher.

Search engines (automated computer programs that scan for a specific term or subject) are the Web's

Popular Search Engines

Yahoo!	*http://www.yahoo.com*	Has a variety of features and is easy to use.
Altavista	*http://www.altavista. digital.com*	Powerful search engine based on indexing of text in Web pages.
Excite	*http://www.excite.com*	Also offers reviews of many websites.
Overture Services	*http://www.overture. com*	Easy-to-use interface with high-quality search filters that allow for specific subject searches.
Lycos	*http://www.lycos.com*	Powerful search engine that can be customized.
WebCrawler	*http://webcrawler.com*	Excellent for simple searches. Very fast.
HotBot	*http://www.hotbot.com*	Very fast engine. Allows beginners to create complex subject searches with a few simple clicks.
Google	*http://www.google.com*	Image Search function enables users to quickly and easily find electronic images relevant to a wide variety of topics. Offers users the ability to search for numerous non-HTML files such as PDF, Microsoft Office, and Corel documents. Direct access to 3 billion web documents.
Ask Jeeves	*http://www.ajkids.com/*	Uses sophisticated language-processing software to understand and match users' questions to an extensive database consisting of thousands of question templates and millions of researched answer links to websites.

cyberbloodhounds—ferreting out websites based upon a keyword or phrase. Each search engine has its own particular strengths and weaknesses. The most popular are listed on page 12.

CYBERSEARCHES

Each search engine contains specific instructions for conducting Web searches. To conduct an efficient search, always try to be as specific as possible—otherwise you will have to sort through long lists! Say you want to obtain information about establishing a nature trail. Typing in the keyword "nature" will return hundreds (if not thousands) of websites dealing with a variety of subjects not even closely related to nature trails. Adding specificity by combining keywords with quotation marks, such as "nature trail construction" will greatly narrow the list. The Appendix lists a number of science supply companies that offer inexpensive probewear—some with connectivity to Palm and other handheld PDA (personal digital assistant) devices.

RECORDING, ANALYZING, AND REPORTING DATA

Data sets are unbiased information gathered through the scientific process that can lead to knowledge and understanding. To be useful, data must be recorded, organized, graphed, analyzed, and reported.

RECORDING DATA

Recording data can be done manually through the reading of an instrument, such as a thermometer, and writing down measurements in a notebook. There are inexpensive probes (temperature, pH, dissolved oxygen, humidity, and more) that will automatically sample and store data. Some probes can be linked to a computer and the data downloaded (transferred). Some probes are commonly available at electronic stores; they are usually battery-operated and can be easily taken into the field. Other digital recording probes are unique because they can be programmed via computer to sample data at either rapid or slow rates depending upon the requirements of the investigation. See Learn More About It to discover just what these probes can do and how to obtain them.

At times, your investigation may require the use of a video or photo camera to record visual information. Try to include some dimensional reference (a ruler or other feature) in your shots to provide the correct perspective. Waterproof, disposable 35 mm cameras are available for use in the field. Digital photo cameras and scanners allow you to capture images and manipulate them in a computer. These digital images can be e-mailed as JPEG files to friends or posted on websites over the Internet.

ORGANIZING DATA

Make sure data sets presented in tables are listed in correct relation to each other. Sometimes your investigations may call for the collection of very large data sets. One way to manage this pile of data is through a *database*—a large, complex list of facts and information. A database can be a card file or an electronic program that can both recall and merge data. *FileMaker Pro* (by FileMaker, Inc., formerly Claris Corporation) is a powerful database program that combines advanced data management and desktop-to-Web network publishing capabilities in a database system. See Learn More About It to discover just how this and other software programs can help you manage data.

GRAPHING DATA

When you make a graph, the first step is to determine what kind to create. What you want to show and the kind of data you have determine which graph is most useful. A *circle graph* is useful in showing parts or proportions of a whole. A *bar graph* is useful for comparing quantities and changes over time. A *line graph* is good for comparing two sets of data or for showing changes and trends over time. There are inexpensive commercial "utility" computer programs such as *GraphMaster* and *Graphical Analysis* that can create standard or custom graphs. See Learn More About It to discover just what these software programs can do to help you display information relationships.

DATA ANALYZING

When you analyze data, you look for trends or patterns. You also look to see whether or not your data support your reasoned guess—your hypothesis. If you have access to a computer, specialized data analysis programs or spreadsheets can help you tabulate, manipulate (perform mathematical computations), and graph your data. Programs such as *Microsoft Excel* or *Lotus 1-2-3* can spare you the drudgery of repetitive calculations and graphing. See Learn More About It to discover just what these software programs can do. These programs may already be available on your home or school computer. Check with your science teacher or school librarian.

REPORTING DATA

Reporting your findings in a clear and concise manner is critical to your success as a young scientist. Scientists communicate their findings (conclusions) to others through published reports, talks, or poster sessions.

Your project report should contain the following parts in this order:

I. Problem statement   The question(s) that your project addresses.

II. Background   All the information that relates to the question. Include a bibliography with at least three sources.

III. Hypothesis   A possible answer to your question or a prediction of what you think might occur.

IV. Experimental Design & Procedure   A description of how you will test your hypothesis. Include all the steps that you will follow. You can include drawings or pictures to help in this explanation. List all the materials used to conduct your experiment(s). Make sure that you design controlled experiments and can identify the variable or variables in each experiment.

V. Results   A listing of all data collected after completion of the experiment(s). Use charts, graphs, statistics, pictures, or drawings to help organize data for easier interpretation. Some experiments should include notes that include time, dates, and other conditions.

VI. Conclusion   An interpretation of your results, generally written in a paragraph.

Be very neat. The report should be word processed, typed, or written clearly in blue or black ink.

PROJECT DISPLAY

Presenting and displaying your project at school will usually require the construction of a display board. Use Figure 1 as a guide to constructing and organizing a typical project display. The following materials are appropriate for constructing the board: 1/4-inch plywood, Peg Board, corrugated cardboard, or thin wafer board. If you build your own display, don't make it too heavy because someone will have to carry it. You can also buy a display board that is already put together. Most education stores or science supply companies sell display boards for a reasonable cost.

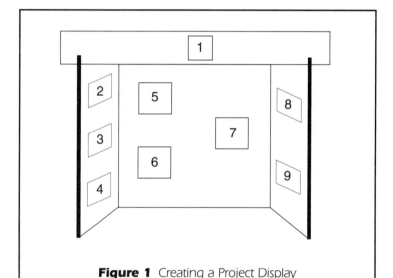

Figure 1 Creating a Project Display
A typical project display should include (1) project title, (2) problem statement, (3) background information, (4) hypothesis, (5) experimental design, (6) procedures, (7) data results: graphs, tables, and photograph, (8) result summary, and (9) conclusion. Make sure all presented information is concise and clearly presented.

SAFETY—THE MOST IMPORTANT ASPECT OF ANY PROJECT

The most important ingredient for success is safety.

1. Be serious about science. A casual or laid-back attitude can be dangerous to you and to others.
2. Read instructions carefully before proceeding with any project outlined in this book. Discuss your experimental procedure with a knowledgeable adult before you begin. A flaw in your design could produce an accident. *Caution: When in doubt, check with a science teacher or a knowledgeable adult.*
3. Keep your work area clean and organized. Never eat or drink while conducting experiments.
4. Respect all life-forms. Never mishandle any vertebrate. Never perform an experiment on a vertebrate that will injure or harm it. Ask your teacher for a copy of any special school guidelines that must be followed when using vertebrates in science fairs.
5. Wear protective goggles when working with liquids or performing an experiment.
6. Do not touch chemicals with your bare hands unless instructed to do so. Do not taste chemicals or chemical solutions. Do not inhale vapors or fumes from any chemical or chemical solution.
7. Clean up chemical spills immediately. If you spill anything on your skin or clothing, rinse it off immediately with plenty of water. Then report what happened to a responsible adult.
8. Keep flammable liquids away from heat sources.
9. Always wash your hands after conducting experiments with any microorganism. Dispose of contaminated waste or articles properly.

BACTERIA— THEY'RE EVERYWHERE!

Bacteria, invisible to the naked eye except in large concentrations (called *colonies*), can be found in every environment on, in, and above Earth: within soil and ocean sediments; in the air; in and on plants and animals from fleas to elephants; and, of course, in and on human beings. Bacteria live on our skin, in our mouths, and in our intestines.

We tend to think that bacteria are only harmful, causing disease, discomfort, and sometimes death. Although some bacteria do cause all these things, most of the time we are not conscious of how bacteria affect our lives. For example, bacteria keep our skin clean and help us digest our food.

On a larger scale, bacteria are fundamental to the continued existence of life on Earth. The number of environments (microhabitats) available to bacteria (and other microorganisms—fungi and protists) far surpasses those available to plants and animals. Bacteria are uniquely

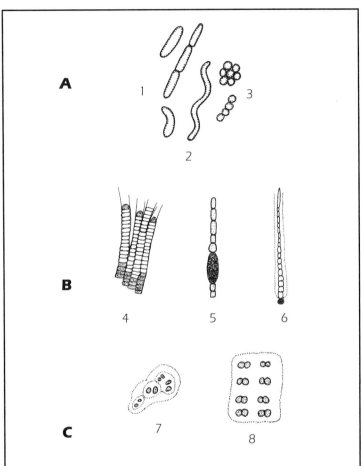

FIGURE 2 Recognizing Bacteria

Most bacteria are the smallest of living cells. Many require the application of a stain to be clearly observed at high magnifications (> 430X). Cells appear in varied arrangements: (A) single cells (rods—straight and curved (1), spirals (2), spheres (3) in chains or in small groups; (B) larger microscopic cells linked together to form hairlike threads or filaments ((4) *Phormidium,* (5) *Anabaena,* and (6) *Gloeotrichia*) that can be observed by the naked eye; and (C) larger microscopic cells within a clear jellylike material forming mats or scums ((7) *Gloeocapsa* and (8) *Merismopedia*) that are visible to the eye.

adapted to exploit these habitats because of their small size and their ability to increase their own kind at phenomenal rates. Bacteria produce or process the gases present in our atmosphere (including oxygen, nitrogen, methane ammonia, and hydrogen) and feed on organic wastes such as the remains of dead organisms. In this manner, bacteria (such as the purple bacteria *Nitrosomonas* and *Nitrobacter* and the nitrogen-fixer *Rhizobium*) are the major recyclers of the chemical components of life.

Although bacteria are very simple organisms, like the rest of life on Earth they must compete and reproduce to survive. Most bacteria exist in three shapes—rods, spheres, and spirals. Another major group, the cyanobacteria (the blue-green algae), is made up of much larger organisms, many existing as long filaments, whose colonies are visible to the naked eye. Almost everyone has observed cyanobacteria as the green, mosslike strands attached to rocks in brooks and streams. Some cyanobacteria, like *Spirulina* and *Anabaena*, are raised commercially for food and as a source of vitamins. Figure 2 shows a variety of bacteria types.

VIEWING THE SUBVISIBLE WORLD

Because most bacteria cannot be seen unless they are in large groups, you will have to provide a suitable microhabitat in which they can grow and flourish. For example, boiled carrots are an excellent medium for *Bacillus megatherium*, a very large, rod-shaped bacterium.

To make carrot media[1], cut carrot pieces and boil

---

1 Nutrient agar plates can be substituted for home-prepared carrot growth medium. See Figure 6 to learn how to pour media plates using prepared, sterile growth media. The Appendix lists sources for prepared growth media.

them for 20 minutes. Use kitchen tongs that have been sterilized in boiling water to place the boiled carrots (allowed to cool) on some dampened towels in a glass bowl. Cover the bowl with clear plastic food wrap. Let your culture incubate at room temperature for a few days in indirect light.

What kinds of growth do you see? Do colonies appear fuzzy, or wet and shiny? (The fuzzy growths are fungi.) From what you observe, do you have more than one type of bacteria colony?

- Use the carrot media technique to sample other bacteria growing on various surfaces, including countertops, plant leaves, books, and soil. Keep notes on the appearance and color of the colonies you isolate. Rub a cotton swab over the surface, then carefully swab the surface of the carrot to inoculate the bacteria.

  If you have a microscope, you can study individual bacterium cells from these colonies. To see individual bacterium cells, you will need to stain them on a microscope slide with a biological stain such as 0.1 percent crystal violet stain, available from your science teacher. Use Figure 3 as a guide for preparing stained slides.

  Observe the slide under a microscope at 430X. Draw what you observe[2]. Can you observe spheres and spirals as well as rods? Make careful notes on the appearance of the colonies where the bacteria you stained came from.

---

2 At 430X, most bacteria will appear as small "specs." For best viewing, scan the edges of stained areas first under low power (100X) and then switch to as high a magnification as possible. Oil immersion magnification (960X) is best for viewing most bacteria.

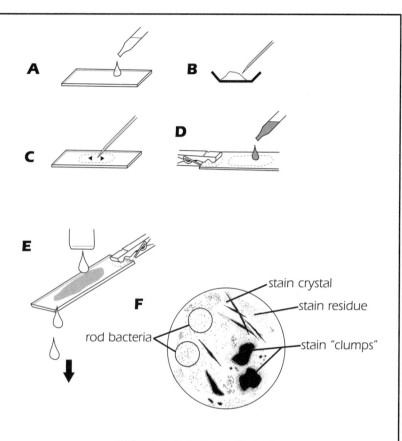

FIGURE 3 Staining Bacteria
(A) Apply a drop of water to a clean microscope slide. (B) With a toothpick or cotton applicator, pick up a small amount of colony or swipe a surface to collect bacteria. (C) Create a smear by mixing the material with the drop of water. Allow the smear to dry. (D) Hold the slide with a clothespin and apply the stain drop by drop until you create a puddle over the smear. (E) After a minute, rinse the stain away over a sink by allowing drops of water to fall on the slide. (F) Observe under a compound microscope at high power (430X). When observing stained smears, begin your search for bacteria cells at a low magnification (e.g. 100X), looking for an area that is NOT heavily stained. Once you find an area rich in bacteria cells, switch to a higher magnification to view them more closely.

- Try other culture media, such as milk left open to air at room temperature and boiled foods such as potatoes and apples. Does each of these media allow growth of the same microorganisms if not directly inoculated?
- Try swabbing (using a cotton applicator) water samples from ponds, puddles, and other sources onto carrot or potato media. Do you observe different bacteria colonies from those you observed before?
- If you have access to a microscope with an oil immersion objective, you can make a hanging-drop preparation to observe how bacteria move. See Chapter 4 for details.

BACTERIA AND UNDERCOOKED FOOD

All raw food has bacteria on its surface. Given the right environmental conditions, a few bacterial cells can explode into invisible and potentially harmful biofilms. If food is contaminated with coliforms—certain types of *Escherichia coli* bacteria—ingestion can cause a critical condition called *gastroenteritis*, the inflammation of the stomach and intestine. *E. coli* is a normal inhabitant of the intestines of all animals, including humans. Normally, *E. coli* serves a useful function in the body by suppressing the growth of harmful bacterial species and by synthesizing appreciable amounts of vitamins. Some *E. coli* strains, such as *E. coli* O157:H7, are capable of causing human illness by producing chemical toxins that cause severe damage to the lining of the intestine.

To guard against ingestion of harmful bacteria, it is important that all foods be well cooked, and generally stored at temperatures lower than 7.2° C (45° F) or heated to temperatures warmer than 60° C (140° F).

- Use a food thermometer, available at most grocery stores, to monitor surface and internal temperatures of food. Create "food heating curves" for various types of food—hot dogs, hamburgers, etc.—during the process of preparation and cooking. Monitor both internal and external temperatures. Do all foods have identical heating curves? Does thickness contribute to lower internal temperatures? Are the pink centers of meats warmer or cooler than 60° C (140° F)?
- With an adult's permission, conduct a survey of internal temperatures of various types of purchased cooked foods to see if these foods pass the 60° C (140° F) threshold.

BACTERIA LIFESTYLES

Bacteria have diverse lifestyles. Microbiologists classify bacteria based upon how they respond to oxygen and how they get their food.

Aerobic bacteria are oxygen lovers that thrive in the presence of oxygen; they are found anywhere there is air. Other bacteria are *anaerobic* and cannot tolerate gaseous oxygen; it kills them. They live in deep underwater sediments or cause bacterial food poisoning. They produce spores that may live in improperly canned food. If the food lacks oxygen, the spores can become active bacteria that secrete poisons into the food. The third group are the "switch-hitters," or *facultative anaerobes*, which prefer growing in the presence of oxygen, but can continue to grow without it.

Some bacteria make their own food by breaking down complex molecules in the environment—they cause rot. Others chemically process specific compounds, like sugar, in a process called *fermentation*. Still others, *photosynthe-*

sizers, which are fueled by light energy, carry out *photo-synthesis* (make their own food) using water or other chemicals such as sulfur and nitrogen.

IS PHOTOSYNTHESIS JUST FOR PLANTS?

Plants use light energy captured by the green pigment chlorophyll to produce food, a process called photosynthesis. Three major events occur in photosynthesis: (1) Light energy from the sun is absorbed by chlorophyll pigments, (2) this light energy is converted to chemical energy, and (3) this chemical energy is stored as sugars. Oxygen gas is a by-product of these light-dependent reactions. Since oxygen is a by-product of photosynthesis, you can detect the presence of photosynthesis by measuring oxygen levels.

Since ancient times, many groups of photosynthetic bacteria have abounded on Earth: the green sulfur, purple sulfur, purple nonsulfur, brownish nonsulfur, and blue-green cyanobacteria.

Hunt along the edges of streams and ponds for small bubbles, signs of oxygen production. Do you see any plants nearby? Is there anything that looks like green threads (filament algae)? Look for colored (blue-green or green) strands attached to rocks or concrete. Collect some algae in a jar or test tube and take it back to your home or school lab. If you don't have access to a stream or pond, try to get some blue-green algae from a store that sells aquarium animals. Examine a wet mount preparation of some strands of collected algae under a microscope to determine whether your algae are filamentous protists or cyanobacteria. Make a wet mount (see Chapter 4) of your collected samples. Examine them under at least a 100X microscope. Cyanobacteria are *prokaryotes*—they have cells without nuclei; their blue-green pigment is seemingly distributed through cells. Green algae (protists) are *eukaryotes*—they have cells with a nucleus; their green pigments are contained in tiny cell structures called *chloroplasts*. Use Figure 2 as a guide to various cyanobacteria and Figure 14 as a guide to some filamentous protists.

Separate the collected algae into two jars or test tubes along with collected water. Put one in the dark and one in the light. What happens after a day or so? Examine the algae under a microscope. Draw what you see. Would you be surprised to know that these organisms are bacteria or protists and not plants? Do some reading on cyanobacteria (blue-green algae) and on green algae.

- Is it correct to define plants as organisms that photosynthesize? Should scientists reclassify plants as a form of bacteria or protist? Do all bacteria and protists perform photosynthesis?
- Experiment with different colors of light and different temperatures on the photosynthesizing ability of the microlife forms you collected. Wrap colored acetate sheets around the jars or test tubes and place on a well lit windowsill. Which light colors allow for greatest photosynthetic activity—the production of the largest number of oxygen bubbles?
- Do cyanobacteria and filamentous protists perform any useful function in aquariums, ponds, or streams?
- Find out whether cyanobacteria live in the ocean, in soil, on trees, or on stones in damp places. Then figure out why they do or do not live in these places.
- Do some reading on phosphate pollution. What does *biodegradable* mean? Check out the claims of manufacturers who say that their soaps are biodegradable. Can you design an experiment that investigates biodegradability?

SETTING UP A MICROBIAL GARDEN—A WINOGRADSKY COLUMN

It is possible to establish a microbial garden of photosynthetic bacteria in a *Winogradsky column*, a device based on a more elaborate one made by Russian microbiologist Sergei Winogradsky, who lived in Russia and France in the early part of the twentieth century.

What You Need
Clear plastic 1-liter soda bottle
Two or three handfuls of sand or mud from an outdoor freshwater or marine source, especially from a marshy area (if possible, collect both types).
Plastic wrap
Rubber band
Hard-boiled egg yolk (as a sulfur source)
Shredded paper (a piece of newsprint about 4 in. × 4 in. or 100 cm²)
Water from the collection source

What To Do

Use Figure 4 as a guide.

1. Carefully remove the neck of the soda bottle using tin snips.
2. Mix the sand or mud with 15 milliliters (1 tablespoon) of egg yolk. Add shredded paper to each sediment type. Mix well.
3. Layer sand and mud in the bottle.
4. Pour water from the collection source over the top of the sand-mud mixture so that there is a small amount of unabsorbed water on top.

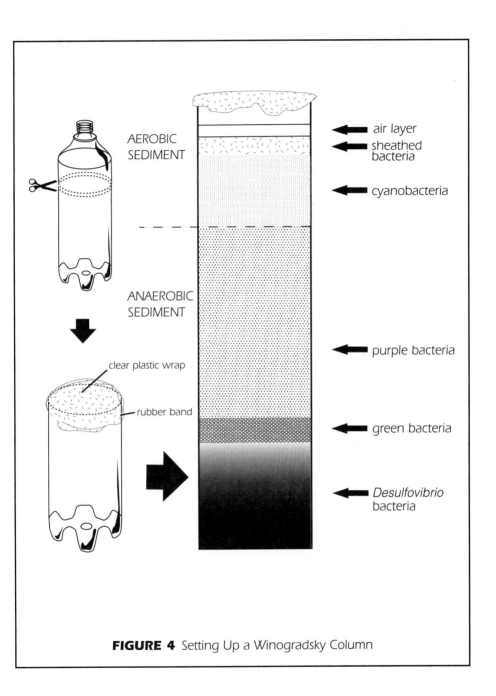

FIGURE 4 Setting Up a Winogradsky Column

5. Cover the bottle with plastic wrap secured by a rubber band and place it in a sunny window.

A rich culture of photosynthetic bacteria will develop within a few weeks. A similar column kept in the dark will also develop a bacterial population, but the bacteria will not be photosynthetic.

Watch the column(s) over several months. Various microenvironments—favoring aerobic, anaerobic, and facultative growth conditions—will be established. Color changes indicate that ecological succession is taking place.

- Observe the changes you see taking place over a period of several months. Record observations every one or two weeks in your notebook. Use colored pencils to illustrate various observed color patterns. Look for colored zones in your Winogradsky column indicating various bacterial populations. Use Figure 2 as a guide in identifying various microbe communities.
- Ask your science teacher to lend you a Pasteur pipet and bulb. Use the long, thin, portion to sample various sediment layers and standing water.
  - Place a drop of a sample on a piece of litmus or pH paper. Record the pH. Are there certain layers that are more acidic than others?
  - Examine other sample drops microscopically. Stain and observe them under as high a magnifying power as possible using a compound microscope. Use Figure 3 as a guide in staining bacteria. Can you observe different kinds (shapes and sizes) of bacteria?
- How is a Winogradsky column similar to the bottom of a pond? How is it different?
- Visit marshes near where you live. Do you smell rotten eggs? What does that tell you about the types of

bacteria in marsh sediments? Do some research on the Web to learn more about marsh gas (hydrogen sulfide [H_2S] gas).

- In 1975, scientists discovered that magnetic fields affect some bacteria. Use a bar magnet to attract magnetotactic bacteria in the column that was kept in the dark. Try the North Pole, then the South Pole. Position one end of a magnet against the glass (where the water is, not the sediment) and hold it there for 15 to 30 minutes. Use a hand lens to determine if any bacteria congregate (white patch) in response to your magnet.
  - Can you concentrate bacteria using multiple bar magnets?
  - Could you concentrate all the magnetotactic bacteria in your column by wrapping a coil of wire around the jar to create an electromagnet using a battery?

SOIL BACTERIA

Just think: 5 milliliters (1 teaspoon) of garden soil contain billions of bacteria! The microcapillary spaces between soil grains hold water films and countless microlife forms, including bacteria. Soil bacteria are critical in recycling materials.

Sample various soil microhabitats by burying glass microscope slides. Over time bacteria, inhabiting the water films will colonize (grow on) the surface of the glass.

Bury glass microscope slides at various depths in soil and mark their locations and depths with small stakes and labeled tags. After a few weeks, carefully dig them up, wrap them in facial tissue, and transport them back to your lab. Wipe off one side with facial tissue and stain the other side. Although most of the dirt particles will be washed off, there will still be plenty of bacteria to see! Use Figure 3 as a guide in staining recovered bacterial biofilms on the glass slides. Observe stained slides under a microscope.

- If you do not have a microscope, you can make replica impressions by carefully pressing the soil-covered side of the microscope slide to the surface of carrot (or potato) media to transfer bacteria from the glass slide to the media. Be careful not to touch the media to any other surface.
- Bury slides in plant pots and then plant corn or other seeds on top of or near them. Use a control. After a few weeks, carefully remove the slides from the growing root systems. Do you observe different bacteria populations on slides buried in pots with and without plants?
- Try burying slides in orchards during the fall. Bury slides just underneath the soil below trees and away from where fruits can fall. Do you notice any change in bacterial populations between the two slide groups? If you do, what do you suppose causes the change?
- Try the following technique on lawns: Examine buried slides both before and after application of fertilizer or pesticide. *Caution: Be sure to wash your hands after handling any soil that has come into contact with any chemical.*
  - What changes do you observe? What effect does applying such chemicals have on the environment? How deep do these chemicals penetrate? How deep does salt applied to road surfaces penetrate soils and affect soil bacteria?

- Does drought affect bacterial growth?
- Do human activities have an effect on soil bacteria?

BACTERIA AS FOOD

Legend has it that yogurt and sour cream were discovered when ancient peoples tasted milk left out in the sun in hot Middle Eastern countries like Turkey and Syria.

- Make your own sour milk, yogurt, kefir (a kind of liquid yogurt), sour cream, or buttermilk.

    You can buy microorganism seed cultures or make your own. For example, a glass of milk left out for 24 hours is an excellent trap for fermenting bacteria and fungi. Or you can make yogurt by adding a spoonful of commercial yogurt labeled as containing active culture, to a can of condensed milk. See if you can duplicate the conditions under which people in ancient cultures first might have discovered these foods. *Caution: Do not taste or eat any of these foods unless you are working under the close supervision of a science teacher who says they are safe to try.*

- Use a toothpick to mix a small amount of yogurt with a drop of water on a clean glass microscope slide. Stain the slide, using Figure 3 as a guide. Observe your stained preparation at a minimum of 430X. How many different types of bacteria can you find?
    - Why is buttermilk needed when baked goods are made with baking soda?
    - Investigate *Acidophilus* milk.

THE TYNDALL EFFECT

In 1872, the English scientist John Tyndall observed that extremely small particles, invisible to the naked eye, could be made visible when a powerful beam of light was passed through air in a darkened room. The presence of particles of a size greater than 100 nanometers[3] causes the light to be scattered in all directions. This is called the Tyndall effect. Since most bacteria are at least 1 or 2 micrometers in diameter, you can use the Tyndall effect to observe bacterial growth without a microscope.

Fill a 1-liter or 1-quart mason jar two-thirds full of water and add some pieces of dried dog food. Let the jar stand undisturbed for one or two days. What happens in the jar?

Fill another mason jar to the same level with water. Place both jars in a darkened room and shine a flashlight at an angle on the side of the first jar. What do you see? Do the same with the second jar. Compare your observations. Now look at the contents of each jar using a hand lens.

Can you observe the Tyndall effect in a darkened room with slightly parted curtains?

FURTHER EXPERIMENTS

Quantify your observations of bacterial populations by constructing a series of "counting screens"—patterns of dots on transparent sheets. Use Figure 5 as a guide. Each screen has a different density (*optical thickness*) that is compared to the turbidity inside the jar. Photocopy the set of screens in Figure 5 onto a sheet of clear acetate. Place the sheet behind the mason jar while making a visual observation. Observe which numbered screen is obscured by the population of floating bacteria particles. For example,

---

3 Nanometer (nm); 100 nm = 1/10 of a micrometer (μm); 1 micrometer = 1/1,000 of a millimeter.

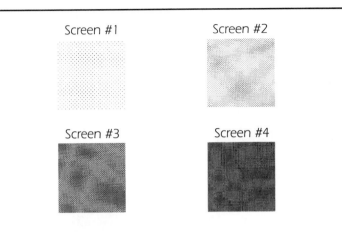

FIGURE 5 Optical Counting Screens
Photocopy these graphics onto the center area of a clear acetate sheet. Place the copied acetate sheet behind a culture jar. Observe the culture jar directly in front on you in strong side light. Screens that are obscured from view indicate a comparable optical density—i.e., Screen #2 has 2X the dots-per-inch (dpi) than Screen #1. Screen #4 has 2X dpi than Screen #3, which has 2X dpi of Screen #2.

if screen #4 is obscured, then the bacterial population is four times greater than what would be necessary to obscure screen #1. Use this optical screen method to get a better idea of the relative population density of bacterial populations in the following experiment.

- Place hay or dried lawn clippings in two 1-liter or 1-quart mason jars. Fill with bottled water. Place the two jars in a 4-liter (4-quart) saucepan filled with about 2 liters (2 quarts) of boiling water, and heat until the water in the mason jars boils for one minute. Allow the jars to cool; then put on the canning caps and tighten them. Label one jar Treatment #1 and the other Treatment #2. Set aside the mason jar labeled Treatment #1.

Observe both jars with a flashlight in a darkened room 24 hours later. Record your observations. Repeat the heating of the second jar (labeled Treatment #2) as before. Be sure to loosen the cap before reheating and then tighten it afterward. In 24 hours, repeat the observations and reheat the jar (labeled Treatment #2) a third time. In 24 hours, observe again.

– What do you conclude from your experiment? Are bacteria killed by simply boiling foods or water once? Why or why not? Do some reading on Tyndallization and pasteurization. Are they the same?

– Do commercial products that advertise that they contain "billions of bacteria" for reducing septic tank problems really contain bacteria? Design an experiment to find out. If they do, how are the bacteria supplied, and how do they work? Try adding some oils (cooking oil and/or motor oil) to a mason jar containing a pinch of one of these products. Are the oils digested? What other commercial uses might there be?

Caution: Don't forget to wash your hands after each session of experimentation.

A CLOSER LOOK AT ANTIBACTERIAL AGENTS

An *antibacterial agent* is an agent (chemical compound or a physical force, like radiation) that can kill or inhibit the growth of bacteria.

GARLIC—ANTIBACTERIAL OR JUST SMELLY?

For centuries, people have believed that garlic has medicinal properties. For example, grave diggers burying victims of the plague in France in 1721 supposedly escaped infection by drinking a concoction of garlic and wine. Today, the same concoction can be bought in French drugstores. Garlic pills are sold in American health-food stores, and magazines such as *Prevention* periodically run articles on the wonders of garlic.

Does garlic have antibacterial properties? Louis Pasteur believed that garlic could kill bacteria. You can answer this question by culturing bacteria using nutrient agar media plates (obtain these from your science teacher or from a biological supply company). Be sure to follow the sterile technique instructions your science teacher gives or those provided with the material.

Use Figure 6 as a guide for casting (pouring) agar plates. Unscrew the media tube a half turn and melt the agar in a microwave—about one minute on a low-power setting. After the agar has melted, allow the tube to cool until it can be held in your hand. Pour half the contents into a sterile petri dish by carefully raising the lid. Pour the remainder into another petri dish. Allow the agar poured into the dishes to solidify.

You will be conducting bacterial sensitivity disk tests. These tests will show how effective a particular substance is in controlling a bacteria population. Use a paper punch to punch 6-millimeter (0.25-in.) paper disks out of construction paper. Use tweezers to dip the paper disks into various test solutions or commercial products. Before you apply the disks to the agar surface, inoculate the agar plate by first touching a cotton swab on the counter surface and then *lightly* rubbing it on the agar surface of a media plate. You can also use a flat-end toothpick to collect bacteria

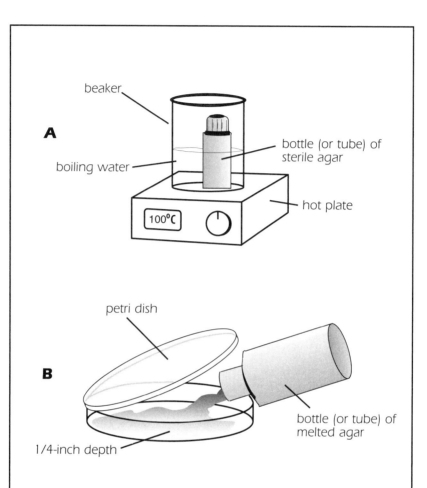

FIGURE 6 Pouring an Agar Plate

(A) Melting agar using a water bath. Melt sterile agar in a glass or plastic media bottle or tube by first loosening the cap and then placing it in either a water bath or in a microwave. (B) Pouring agar plates. Allow the media tube or bottle to cool so that it can be held in your hand. Pour the contents into a petri dish to a depth of 1/4-inch. Close the cover and allow the agar to harden. Store poured plates upside down to prevent condensation forming on the agar surface. A media tube will pour 2 plates; a media bottle will pour 7 to 8 plates.

colonies already isolated on your carrot (or other food) media. Place the disks equidistant from one another in a circle, as shown in Figure 7. After 2 or 3 days of incubation at room temperature, measure the *zone of inhibition* (the clear area around a disk) to determine which applied substance has spread out into the agar and is most effective. The greater the zone of inhibition, the more effective an antibacterial agent.

Run sensitivity tests on various commercial antibacterial products such as Triclosan in soap solutions, dishwashing liquids, cleaners, and household disinfectants. Is household bleach an effective antibacterial agent?

Examine various plant materials or by-products with the following experiments:

- Crush or boil garlic to extract its juice. Use tweezers to dip paper disks in the liquid. After the paper disks dry, apply them to the agar surface. Arrange the disks on the agar surface so that they are equidistant from one another.
- Perform sensitivity tests using garlic tablets. Dissolve a garlic tablet of known weight in a known volume of water. Record the "strength" of the garlic solution by dividing the weight of the tablet (in grams) by the volume of water (in milliliters). For example, a 60-mg tablet dissolved in 30 mL of water would yield a garlic solution with a strength of 2 mg/mL.
- Test other close "relatives" of garlic—leeks, onions, shallots, and turnips. Do any of these plant juices, boiled or not, have antibacterial properties?
- Test other herbs and spices. Which method of preparation is most effective: grinding to extract juice, boiling, or crushing tablet form?
- Is a combination of agents more effective (does it have

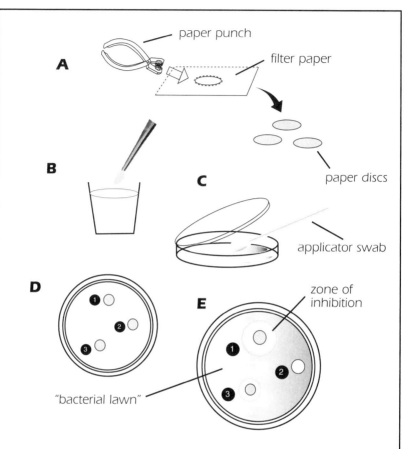

FIGURE 7 Sensitivity Testing

(A) Use a paper punch to punch out filter paper (or construction paper) discs. (B) Use a forceps to immerse paper discs in various test solutions. (C) Create a "bacterial lawn" by using a sterile applicator swab to pick up bacterial colonies from an existing culture or from a surface. Swab the entire surface of the plate. (D) Use forceps to place moist paper discs onto the agar surface. Record their positions on the plate as well as test solution in your notebook. (E) Following 3-5 days incubation, inspect for "zones of inhibition" or an area of no bacterial growth around paper discs. (1) Large zone of inhibition demonstrates significant inhibitory effect. (2) Smaller zone of inhibition demonstrates some inhibitory effect. (3) No zone of inhibition, no inhibitory effect on bacterial growth.

a greater zone of inhibition) than single substances alone?

HEAVY METALS

More than one hundred years ago, physicians used to administer mercury compounds to cure venereal diseases. Can trace amounts of heavy metals, like mercury, really kill bacteria?

Clean three 1- to 2-cm (0.5-in.) metal disks (try copper, aluminum, and sheet metal disks) one at a time and place them on the agar as soon as they are clean.

1. Wash the disks with soap and water.
2. Place the disks in a cup containing rubbing alcohol.
3. Dip tweezers in the alcohol (to kill any bacteria on them) and remove the disks one at a time.

Allow the discs to air-dry and then apply them to the agar surface.

Use a ruler to measure any zones of inhibition around the discs that metal ions spreading out into the agar may have caused. Record your results in your notebook. Did the metal ions react with the growing bacteria?

- Read about the toxicity of different metals. Are some metals more toxic than others? Can you explain?
- Visit your local pharmacy and read the ingredient labels of over-the-counter antibiotic ointments or creams. Can you find any heavy-metal compounds listed? Look for zinc, copper, and other metal-element compounds.

Caution: After your experiments, wash your hands with soap and hot water. Pour a small amount of rubbing alcohol onto the agar plate surfaces and let sit for at least 30 minutes before discarding. Be sure to decontaminate all instruments as well.

A CLOSER LOOK AT NITROGEN-FIXING BACTERIA

Some bacteria are specialists. Some generate methane gas, while others digest petroleum or secrete powerful toxins that cause illness. Still others, the nitrogen-fixing bacteria, convert atmospheric nitrogen into a form that can be used by plants (ammonia). Other bacteria convert the ammonia into nitrites and nitrates, nutrients essential for plant growth in a series of interrelated processes known as the nitrogen cycle (see Figure 8).

You can investigate these bacteria[4] using clover, a common plant found along roadsides and in fields.

Carefully dig up the clover's root system and wash off the soil. Find the pea-size (or smaller) nodules on the roots. Two colors of nodules can be observed. Pink nodules indicate that *Rhizobium* root nodule bacteria are fixing nitrogen; green nodules indicate that the bacteria are reproducing but not fixing nitrogen. *Rhizobium* begins to fix nitrogen only after it stops reproducing.

Cut off a small piece of a pink nodule and crush it between two microscope slides. Separate the slides and stain using the crystal violet stain method described earlier. Under the microscope (at 430X), you should observe pockets of rod-shaped bacteria in groups of four to eight cells inside a thin membrane.

Find out whether these bacteria are indeed responsible for root nodule formation. Place clover seeds inside folded, damp paper towels. Place the paper towels (and seeds) in a dish and loosely cover them to prevent them

---

4 You can also obtain root nodule bacteria inexpensively from commercial sources (see the Appendix). Simply mix the powdered inoculant (containing *Rhizobium* bacteria) with soil when germinating seeds.

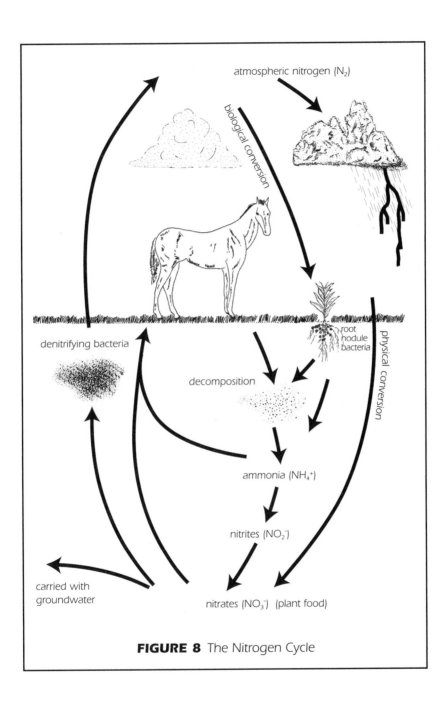

atmospheric nitrogen (N$_2$)

biological conversion

physical conversion

denitrifying bacteria

root hodule bacteria

decomposition

ammonia (NH$_4^+$)

nitrites (NO$_2^-$)

carried with groundwater

nitrates (NO$_3^-$) (plant food)

FIGURE 8 The Nitrogen Cycle

from drying out. Keep the paper towels damp (but not wet). In a few days, the seeds will germinate. When they have developed a root system 2 to 5 centimeters (1 to 2 in.) long, place them in a shallow dish of water. Grind some clover nodules (15 to 30) and inoculate the young clover plants by mixing the ground nodule material in the seedlings' water. You are inoculating (introducing bacteria into) the young clover plants with nitrogen-fixing bacteria contained in the nodules.

Use a control as well—young clover plants inoculated with pieces of a clover root nodule boiled for 30 minutes to kill any bacteria.

Wait a few days and then plant both groups of plants. After two or three months, dig them up and inspect them for nodule formation.

What do you conclude about inoculating other clover plants using nodules? Which are the active ingredients: the nodules themselves or the bacteria inside?

- Read about leguminous plants. Can all plants incorporate nitrogen-fixing bacteria and form nodules?
- How are food crops inoculated with nitrogen-fixing bacteria? Will nodules left in the soil re-inoculate next year's planted crop? Devise a method to inoculate crops.
- Does freezing root nodules affect their ability to inoculate root nodule bacteria into other clover plants?

MICROBES FOR PROFIT

Over the centuries, microbes have been harnessed as microchemical factories to both create and clean up. Almost every day there are new discoveries. For example, the bacterium *Azoarcus tolulyticus* eats toluene—a major hydrocarbon component of gasoline. Isolated from a contaminated aquifer (an underground reservoir of water), it is the first anaerobe toluene-degrading microbe available to environmental scientists. As an anaerobe, this bug breathes nitrogen in the form of nitrate, rather than oxygen. It is hoped that contaminated underground water supplies can be cleaned up (*bioremediated*) by pumping nitrate and *Azoarcus* into the water.

One of nature's toughest microbes is *Deinococcus radiodurans*—able to survive at radiation levels that kill all other living creatures. Today, scientists are devising ways to use this bacterium to clean up radiation-contaminated sites.

Many microbes are packaged for consumer and industrial use. Let's take a closer look at two of them.

BIOPESTICIDES

There are more than ninety species of naturally occurring bacteria that target and kill insects. Introduced in the 1960s, one of the safest insecticides on the market, *Bacillus thuringiensis* (Bt), produces a crystalline protein endotoxin that causes intestinal paralysis in the larvae of some species of insects (mosquitoes, moths, and butterflies). In recent years, scientists have transferred Bt genes to other microbes to produce more potent "bio-bullets" and even plant vaccines, targeting a wider variety of insect pests.

• Visit your local garden center and scan the shelves for products that contain Bt. Most are available as powders that contain spores and toxin crystals (harmless to humans) as well as inert ingredients. Use a wet toothpick to collect and mix a little of the powder with a drop of water on a microscope slide. Can you observe spores and toxin crystals?

• Test the "staying power" of applying Bt powder to

plant-leaf surfaces by using transparent tape to collect surface samples. Press a 5-centimeter (2-in.) length of tape to a leaf surface to which the Bt powder was applied. Remove the tape and reapply it to the surface of a clean microscope slide. Scan the slide for the presence of spores and toxin crystals. Are they present hours, days, and weeks after application? Following a rain? Make separate tape-slide preparations of each of these events.

- Design some experimental trials that test product effectiveness on collected caterpillars. For example, how low a dose is still effective?
- See if you can devise a floating Bt sponge-dispensing system that would protect against mosquito larvae in birdbaths, swimming pools, ponds, etc.

OIL-DEGRADING MICROBES

Consider that just 3.8 liters (1 gallon) of spilled oil can spread to cover 1.6 hectares (4 acres) of water! Consider also that about 15 percent of the volume of any ocean oil spill will eventually come ashore. Since the *Exxon Valdez* spill in March 1989, many commercial products to bioremediate oil spills have been made available. These products usually contain a potpourri of many *petrophilic* (oil-eating) microbes to combat these human-made plagues. Oil-degrading microbes, in a commercial product, are available through one of the sources named in the Appendix.

- Apply a small amount of the commercial product to a simulated oil spill in a small vial. Use a few drops of new motor oil to simulate your spill. Observe what happens to the "spill" over time. If possible, use a pipet to sample the oil layer and observe your sample under a microscope.

- Try simulating beach conditions in a small dish. Use two sizes of aquarium sand to simulate beach sand and gravel. Use small pebbles to simulate beach cobbles. Is the commercial product effective in all shoreline conditions?
- Temperature extremes can reduce the effectiveness of such bioremediation products. With an adult's approval, compare degradation results by placing some experimental setups in a refrigerator and leaving some at room temperature.

FUNGI—
THOSE AMAZING
SCAVENGERS

Fungi are Earth's scavengers. Along with bacteria, they perform an invaluable service, recycling organic material from dead life-forms. They do this by secreting digestive enzymes that break down organic material. Fungi are capable of digesting almost anything, as long as it is in a moist environment.

You are probably familiar with mushrooms. But what you usually see and always eat is just the reproductive part of the fungus itself. The rest of the fungus lies hidden underground in the form of a netlike or cottonlike mass of slender, interwoven tubes called *hyphae*.

Many fungi cause diseases, especially of plants. Gardeners and farmers constantly battle against molds, mildews, and rusts. Many other fungi form mutual relationships with plants, helping to provide recycled organic nutrients to their root systems. Others are used in baking bread and in making alcoholic beverages, industrial chemicals, and medicines.

Fungi reproduce by means of microscopic reproductive bodies called *spores*. Each spore contains a single cell, protected by a thick wall and capable of withstanding temperature extremes for long periods without water. Fungi spores are incredibly light, so they are easily distributed by wind and air currents. Some can stay aloft for months!

Caution: Because many mushrooms are poisonous, never taste or eat any wild mushroom. Do not make the mistake of thinking a mushroom is edible simply because it looks like a mushroom you might find in a supermarket. Many edible mushrooms have poisonous look-alikes.

STALKING THE WILD FUNGUS

Almost everyone is familiar with mushrooms and toadstools (see Figure 9). They are the fruiting bodies of fungi. Mushroom caps are usually suspended by a stem (*stipe*). The rest of the fungus is a network (*mycelium*) made up of hyphae.

Inside each fruiting body is a structure called a *hymenium*, which contains microscopic, clublike structures called *basidia*. Spores are produced in the basidia. In gilled mushrooms, the hymenium is located on the gills. In pore mushrooms, the hymenium is located in tubes that lead to exterior pores. Both gills and pores open to the outside so that spores can be released into the air.

Other mushroom types (puffballs and stinkhorns) do not have gills or pores. These fungi retain their spores, which are not released until the outside body decays or is ruptured. Some fungi form symbiotic (beneficial) associations with trees called mycorrhizae.

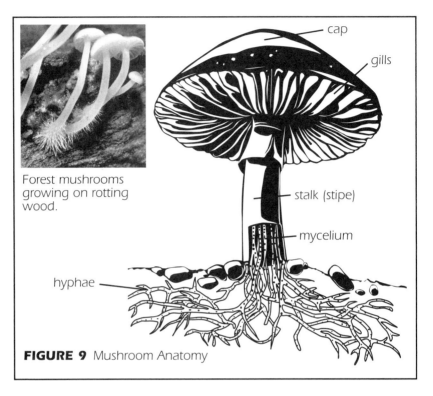

Forest mushrooms growing on rotting wood.

cap

gills

stalk (stipe)

mycelium

hyphae

FIGURE 9 Mushroom Anatomy

Here are a few activities to better acquaint you with fungi.

- Carefully expose the shallow root hair system of almost any wild plant and use a pocket lens to view it. Remove part of the plant's root system (be sure to include small clumps of soil) and place it on top of some black construction paper in strong light. You will see the tiny, transparent, hairlike threads of a fungus at work.
- Go mushroom hunting. Take along a penknife and a hand lens. Look for mushrooms in meadows, in dark and moist places, on rotting logs, on lawns following a rain, or on compost heaps. Use the penknife to care-

fully move soil away from the mushroom's stalk to expose mycelia. Place some mycelia along with soil in a plastic bag to prepare a wet mount in your home or school laboratory to observe under a microscope (at 100X). Use a needle to transfer small pieces to a drop of stain (0.1 percent methylene blue or a drop of fabric dye) to make a wet mount. The stain will help you see individual hyphae clearly.

- You can also make mushroom spore prints, which are helpful in identifying mushrooms. After locating a mushroom that has gills, cut off the stipe at the base of the cap and place it, gill side down, on a piece of white paper. Cover the mushroom cap with a bowl for 4 to 6 hours. The spores will form a print on the paper. To preserve the print, spray it with clear lacquer. Test many different kinds of mushrooms. Are some spore prints all the same color or different colors?

  Examine mushroom spores by using the tip of a toothpick that has been dipped in water. Touch the tip of the toothpick to a portion of a spore print. Transfer spores to a drop of water on a clean microscope slide. Add a coverslip and examine the wet mount at 100X under a compound microscope.

- Make a moisture chamber to incubate collected molds. Most molds require high humidity for growth. A slice of bread (especially one made without preservatives) can become a universal growth medium for a variety of collected forms.

  Place a slice of bread on the inside lid of a margarine or frozen whipped topping container and sprinkle 5 to 10 milliliters (1 to 2 tsp.) of water on the bread. Use a cotton swab to "collect" fungi from various sources: tree trunks, surface of soil in a flowerpot, plant leaves, etc. Lightly "swab" the cotton applicator over the surface of the moistened bread to inoculate it. Punch several holes in the bottom of the container and place it upside down on the lid. Observe the container daily with a magnifying glass. Use a clean toothpick to mix a sample of hyphae (cottony material) into a drop of 0.1 percent methylene blue stain (or distilled water) and observe under a compound microscope. Use Figure 3 as a guide for staining fungal hyphae.

- Place a boiled seed (wheat, rice, or corn) in a small dish of water. Over the next week, you should see a mass of hyphae growing on or around the seed. Float

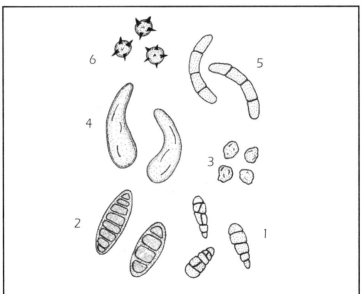

FIGURE 10 Guide to Fungal Spores
(1) *Alternaria*, which causes potato blight and black rot on carrots; (2) Helminthosporium, which causes oat blight; (3) *Penicillium*, the blue-green fruit mold that is a source of penicillin; (4) mushroom spores; (5) *Fusarium*, which causes yellow disease of celery; (6) *Aspergillus*, the common black mold that attacks bread and fruit (400X).

bits of hyphae in a drop of water on a microscopic slide. Try staining the hyphae. Do mold hyphae resemble mushroom hyphae?

- Explore your refrigerator, bread box, or other food storage areas for signs of fungal activity.
- Try to identify the fungi by using the Visual Guide to Fungi Types section later in this chapter. If you can't find any fungi, grow your own, using moistened bread, citrus fruits, or leftovers placed in a sealed plastic bag. Be sure to get your parents' permission before doing this.
- Rain showers bring fungal spores. Attach a loop of sticky tape to a clean microscopic slide. Hold it horizontally to capture the first few drops of a gentle rain. Later, use a microscope to examine the surface of the tape. Use Figure 10 as a guide in identifying the more common fungal spores.
- Design a project to investigate the presence of fungal spores in rain. How did they get there? Are they in only the first drops? If so, why?

COMPOSTING: RECYCLING NATURE'S WAY

Composting is the biological decomposition of organic waste materials under controlled conditions. It was first used by the Romans more than 2,000 years ago to improve the quality of their soil. Today, composting is also used as a way of managing waste. In fact, composting has been classified as a form of recycling. In the past decade, many communities have turned to composting as an environmentally sound and economically feasible solution to waste-disposal problems.

Composting takes place continuously in nature, as plants and animals die and decompose to form humus.

During the process of decomposition, bacteria, fungi, and a few other organisms break down plant and animal remains into simpler components. As a result, the nutrients contained in the bodies of plants and animals are released into the soil, where they can be used by living plants.

Since the full decomposition process in a compost pile takes about six months, you may want to do this project for a science fair or as an ongoing classroom project.

MAKING COMPOST

1. Locate an area in your yard (or the schoolyard) that gets moderate sunshine. See Figure 11 to learn how to construct a compost facility there.
2. Gather materials to be composted. Be mindful always to maintain a 2:1 mixture of carbon to nitrogen. Generally, fresh green plant materials are high in nitrogen, while dried leaves, hay, and brush are high in carbon.
3. During the first 6 weeks, moisten the waste material twice a week using a gentle mist. Turn your compost material over completely using a shovel. Shred the material as you turn it over. (On very hot days, you should turn over your pile twice a day to eliminate odor buildup. Do not add water during rainy weeks.)
4. After this initial "run-in period," allow the compost material to "cure" over a 6-month period to produce a fertilizer that can be added to soil. Compost is ready to use when it is dark brown and crumbly and smells like earth. (Generally, a pile started in the summer or fall should be ready for use the following spring.)

TAKING THE PULSE OF THE PILE

A compost pile is really a recycling factory in miniature. Within, microbes repackage organic and inorganic nutri-

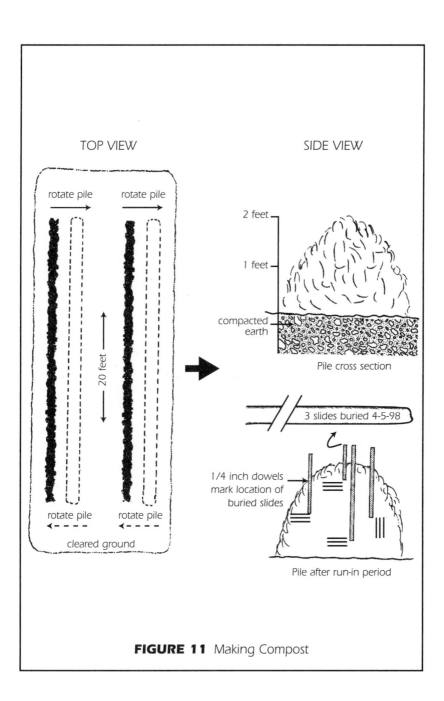

TOP VIEW

SIDE VIEW

rotate pile   rotate pile

2 feet

1 feet

compacted earth

Pile cross section

20 feet

3 slides buried 4-5-98

1/4 inch dowels mark location of buried slides

rotate pile   rotate pile

cleared ground

Pile after run-in period

FIGURE 11 Making Compost

ents locked within the cellular structure of yard waste into usable forms that plants require.

- After the initial run-in period, bury some glass microscope slides at various locations within the pile (see Figure 11). Try not to disturb these areas for at least 6 to 8 weeks. Afterward, carefully remove the glass slides and stain them according to the directions in Chapter 2. (Use paper towels to wipe one side of the glass clean, and then stain the other side.) Observe the slides under high-dry (430X) of a compound microscope. Compile a diversity index (see Chapter 6) for microlife you observe at various depths with the pile. You should take data nearer the outside of the pile (closer to oxygen) and toward the inside of the pile. Slides should be observed at various time periods during compost development. Record your results in your notebook.
- Use a soil test kit (available at lawn care centers) to analyze the nutrient content of your finished product. Does it have measurable amounts of phosphorous, nitrogen, and other nutrients? What is its pH? How does your compost compare to commercial types available locally? Try to take measurements once a week; record your results in your notebook.
- Use a Berlese apparatus or pitfall trap (See Chapter 6) to capture and examine the small invertebrates in your compost.
- Try to get an idea of the total area and volume of biomass (composting material) you initially started with. For example, a small compost pile of 2 feet high and 2 feet wide would have an area of about 4 square feet and a cubic volume of approximately 8 cubic feet (2 feet $\times$ 2 feet $\times$ 2 feet). Generally, this initial compost

volume can shrink 50 percent over time as microbes process it. Based upon these data, design a facility that will compost the leaves and grass clippings for your neighborhood. Research why composting would be a better alternative than landfilling a similar volume of material.

- Would sealing a compost pile make it more effective in decomposing plant materials? For example, what would happen if you staked a plastic sheet over a compost pile to completely cover it?
- Based on your composting studies, can you determine which type of microbe processing—aerobic or anaerobic—is most effective in converting plant material to useful fertilizer? For example, you might try comparing the effect of turning over compost versus not turning it over.
- What type of microbe processing do you think is happening in a landfill? Hint: Almost all landfills produce methane gas. Read up on anaerobic, methane-producing bacteria.

MEASURING THE HEAT OF DECOMPOSITION

Decomposition is a microbe-induced thermal reaction.

- Use a digital thermometer to monitor the temperature of the pile at various levels. Plot and compare temperature readings to those obtained outdoors. Are all areas of the pile equally warmer or colder than outside conditions? Do the rates of temperature change increase when measurements are taken a few hours after the pile is turned?
- Does height affect the pile's core temperature?
- Find out if your local Department of Public Works

has a wood-chip pile. If so, ask if you can take temperature readings. Does a wood-chip pile differ in temperature profile from a compost pile?

- If possible, observe a wood-chip pile early on a cool morning. What do you observe that tells you that the heat of decomposition is at work?

THE SPOILERS OF FOOD

Food-spoiling fungi have three main objectives: (1) to convert their food into more of themselves, (2) to reproduce, and (3) to convert their food into chemicals that will discourage you or other organisms (including other fungi) from eating this food.

- Microbes need at least 20 percent moisture content to grow. For dry grains, legumes, powdered milk, and other low-moisture foodstuff, bacterial spoilage will seldom be a problem as long as the moisture level remains scant. Design experiments that explore this relationship of moisture content and microbial growth and contamination. For example, you might want to place various dry foods inside a moisture chamber (a sealed plastic container containing a damp sponge) to determine at what moisture and temperature levels—measured with a digital relative humidity probe—mold growth first appears. (Retailers on the Web offer digital moisture probes. See the Appendix.)
- Evaluate various food-packaging methods. Are they effective in protecting food inside your moisture chamber?
- Investigate freeze-dried "trail" foods commonly available in sporting or outdoor supply stores. Will these foods spoil if removed from their packages and left

out in room conditions or in a moisture chamber for varied periods of time?

- Use the key in the next section to identify the fungi responsible for food spoilage in your kitchen. Find out whether fungi prefer certain foods or whether certain fungi grow only on certain foods. For example, can you get fungi to grow on very acidic fruits such as lemons more easily than on less acidic apples? Use a moisture chamber to grow some fungi on bread. After you have grown a "crop" of mold, consult the Visual Guide to Fungi Types to identify mold type(s). Then use the tip of a toothpick to collect spores from the mold in the moisture chamber and transfer and inoculate whole or cut fruit pieces such as grapefruit, lemon, apple, and pear. Place the inoculated fruit in the moisture chamber and monitor with a magnifying glass every 6 to 12 hours.

    You may wish to study how fruit that is damaged or bruised in susceptible to fungus. Develop and test a hypothesis that explains your findings.

- Experiment with various foods to see whether any prevent spoilage or kill fungi. Try vinegar, onion or garlic juice, salt, hot pepper, lemon juice, and other foods. Develop your own powerful preserving agent to thwart aggressive fungi.

A VISUAL GUIDE TO FUNGI TYPES

Here is a key you can use to identify fungi. You will need a hand lens or a microscope.

To use the key, begin with statement 1a and proceed until the identification is certain. Note: The spheres referred to below are *sporangia*, reproductive structures of certain fungi. They contain spores.

fungal hyphae
without cross walls—
Deutromycetes

fungal hyphae
with cross walls—
Zygomycetes

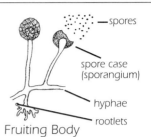

—spores

spore case
(sporangium)

hyphae

rootlets

Fruiting Body

1a Examine your fungus. If there are fuzzy growth
areas colored black, white, and/or gray, **GO TO 2**

1b If there are fuzzy growth areas colored yellow or
blue-green, **GO TO 4**

2a If, under a hand lens, the hyphae are not
readily visible and there are numerous
small spheres, the fungus is
Aspergillus flavus.

2b If, under a hand lens, white to gray hyphae are
readily visible, **GO TO 3**

3a If the hyphae are beige-white and
black spheres are not easily observed,
the fungus is *Mucor.*

3b If the hyphae are gray to white
and black spheres are easily
observed, the fungus is *Rhizopus.*

4a If the hyphae are yellow with numerous dark spheres, the fungus is *Aspergillus niger.*

4b If the hyphae are blue-green to gray and few, if any, dark spheres are observed, the fungus is *Penicillium.*

THE LICHEN—PROTIST OR FUNGUS?

A lichen is a unique "two-kind" organism—a fungus and a protist living together in a mutually beneficial relationship. Figure 12 illustrates the three major lichen types. When hunting for lichens, look for walnut, ash, maple, and ginkgo trees; these are excellent lichen substrates. An excellent reference source for identifying lichens is M.E. Hale's *How to Know the Lichens.*

- Use a razor blade to cut very thin slices from a lichen body. Use a magnifying glass to examine their general structure. Place one slice in a drop of water on a microscope slide. Use sewing needles to tease it apart. Place a coverslip over the separated material. Use a compound microscope to observe which part is fungus and which is protist. What benefit (if any) does each derive in the association? Use Figure 13 as a guide to lichen microanatomy.
- What color pigments can you observe in dried lichens?
- Do lichens normally found growing on tree bark also grow on rocks, or vice versa?

FIGURE 12 Common Lichens—the three major types

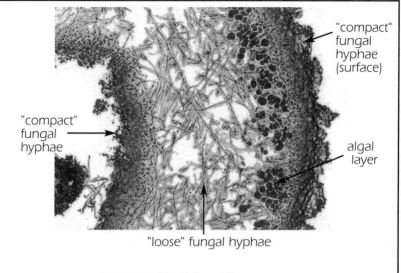

FIGURE 13 Lichen Microantomy
Microscopic cross-section of a lichen. Sunlight is filtered through the compact fungal hyphae surface to reach the photosynthetic algal cells below. The bulk of any lichen body is made up of loosely interwoven fungal hyphae.

- What conditions are ideal for lichen growth? How fast do they grow?
- Can lichens be boiled and the extracts used to dye cloth?

LICHENS AS BIOINDICATORS

Lichens are extremely sensitive to air pollution, especially to sulfur dioxide. This sensitivity is often obvious in urban areas. When parts of trees are close to city traffic, lichens grow only on the side of the tree opposite the traffic flow.

The trunk transect method will help you quantify lichen distribution and gauge lichens' effectiveness as bioindicators of local air quality. With thumbtacks, secure a cloth tape measure around a tree at chest height, with the zero mark facing west. Place colored thumbtacks at the other compass points (north, east, and south). Begin counting lichen species at the west compass point, continuing clockwise to north, and then east and south. Record the species that touch the top of the tape measure at regular increments, such as every 5 centimeters (2 in.). Conduct transects on at least five trees within a given study area. Compute averages for each study area.

- If feasible, try conducting transects in urban, suburban, and outlying countryside settings. Conduct surveys that address these questions: Are lichen populations affected in overall numbers or in diversity (kinds) by environmental influences such as light, wind direction, or proximity to industrial activity? For example, do your transect counts show lichen growing in only one compass direction, such as one that is shielded from prevailing winds?

  To illustrate your findings, make color overlays for a map of the area(s) you surveyed. For example, use different colors to represent lichen types occurring within a geographical area.

- Can you find evidence of lichens, such as *Leparia*, that are pollution-tolerant? Other organisms, such as the protist *Trentepolia*, whose crustlike yellow growth is often visible on moist stones, bark, and leaves, is another indicator of polluted air.

CHAPTER 4

ONE-CELLED ORGANISMS AND OTHER PROTISTS— INHABITANTS OF THE SUBVISIBLE WORLD

They live in pond water; on submerged rocks, aquarium glass, and bark; in soils and beach sands; and even in snow. But you usually can't see them—except through a microscope. They are the protists—organisms usually consisting of one cell and usually capable of moving. Some common freshwater protists are shown in Figure 14.

Although most protists are single cells, they engage in exactly the same life functions as other larger organisms: eating, making their own food, moving about, and selecting partners for reproducing. Protists include the protozoa, algae, slime molds, and seaweeds. They play varied roles in the microworlds they inhabit. Some are scavengers, feeding on dead remains; others feed on bacteria or hunt down other protists; still others make their own food the way green plants do. Certain protists do a combination of all three.

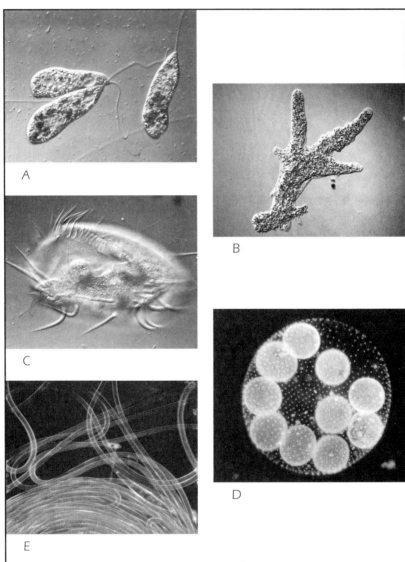

FIGURE 14 Common Types of Freshwater Protists
(A) flagellate (*Euglena sp.*), (B) amoeba (*Amoeba sp.*), (C) ciliate
(*Paramecium sp.*), (D) filament (*Oscillatoria sp.*), and (E) colony
(*Volvox sp.*)

A compound microscope is the best instrument to use for observing these interesting organisms, but a small single-lens microscope can also be used.

MICROSCOPES

You will need a microscope to do some of the projects in this book. For example, you will need a microscope when doing many projects with protists and other microorganisms. For other projects, a microscope would be nice to have. If you are studying butterflies, for instance, you may wish to examine them under a microscope to study their tiny scales. An excellent guide is M. Bleifeld's *Experimenting with a Microscope*.

BUILDING YOUR OWN MICROSCOPE

If you don't have access to a microscope, you can build your own "flea glass." The flea glass is a single-lens microscope adapted from a design by J. Cuff, a well-known eighteenth-century English microscope builder. (One of Cuff's clients was the great Swedish naturalist Carolus Linnaeus, who used a flea glass to aid him in classifying microlife forms.) This simple microscope works on the principle of magnification attained by a single convex lens. A sliding arm is used to adjust the focus. Depending on the curvature of the lens used, the object can be magnified between 10X and 20X—ten to twenty times the object's true size. You should be able to observe protists that are 300 µm[5] (0.012 in.) or larger, like *Paramecium* or *Volvox*. Building a flea glass is a worthwhile

---

5 µ is the symbol for micrometer. 1 µm = 1/1,000,000 of a meter; 1 millimeter (mm) = 1,000 µm.

project in itself. Perhaps you can think of some useful modifications to improve its abilities.

What You Need
Hand or electric drill with 3/4-, 1/4-, and 1/16-inch bits
15 centimeters (6 in.) of 1-inch dowel
White glue
Velcro strip, 1.27 centimeters by 2.54 centimeters (0.5 in by 1 in.)
6.27 centimeters (2.5 in.) of 1/2 inch dowel
3.77 centimeters (1.5 in.) of 1/4 inch dowel
2 rubber bands
Canvas needle 5 centimeters (2 in.) long
20X pocket magnifier

What To Do

To construct the flea glass, use the magnified view shown in Figure 15 as a guide.

1. Drill a 3/4-inch hole through the 1-inch dowel about 5 centimeters (2 in.) from the end.
2. Glue a strip of Velcro to line this hole.
3. Use the rubber bands to attach the pocket magnifier to the drilled end of the 1-inch dowel.
4. Drill a 1/4-inch-diameter hole 1.27 centimeters (0.5 in.) from one end of the 1/2-inch dowel. Drill the hole all the way through the dowel.
5. Drill a 1/16-inch hole in the face cut of one end of the 1/4-inch dowel and insert the canvas needle into this hole.

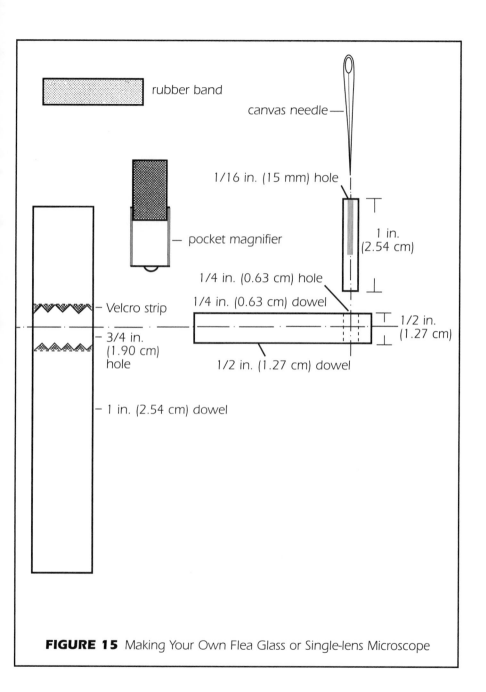

rubber band

canvas needle—

1/16 in. (15 mm) hole

— pocket magnifier

1 in. (2.54 cm)

1/4 in. (0.63 cm) hole

1/4 in. (0.63 cm) dowel

— Velcro strip

— 3/4 in. (1.90 cm) hole

1/2 in. (1.27 cm)

1/2 in. (1.27 cm) dowel

— 1 in. (2.54 cm) dowel

FIGURE 15 Making Your Own Flea Glass or Single-lens Microscope

6. Insert the 1/4-inch dowel into the hole in the 1/2-inch dowel.

7. Insert the 1/2-inch dowel into the 1-inch dowel so that the assembly faces the side where the magnifier is attached.

Figure 16 is a drawing of the completed flea glass, and Figure 17 shows a photograph of the author's flea glass.

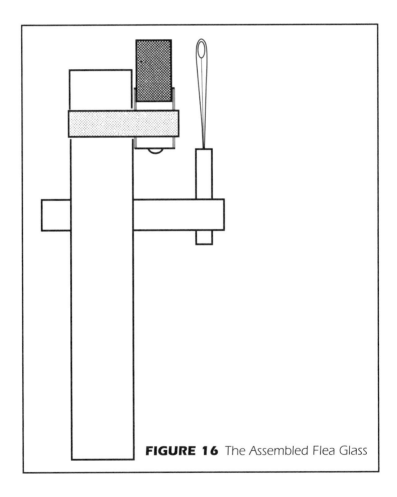

FIGURE 16 The Assembled Flea Glass

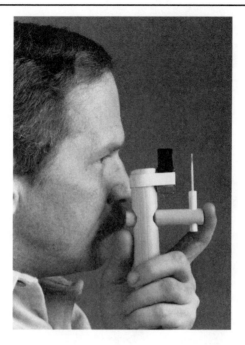

FIGURE 17 The Author's Flea Glass

To use the glass, begin with a point source of illumination, such as a table lamp, about 1 meter (3 ft.) away. Such a light source will give you concentrated light. At times you may want softer lighting sources to increase visual contrast. In that case, use a window, open sunlight, or other light backgrounds for diffused (soft) lighting.

Caution: Never point the lens directly toward the sun. It can damage your eyes.

To pick up water samples, remove the needle and position it in line with the lens by manipulating the dowels. The friction fit of the Velcro should make the instrument easy to focus. See Figure 18.

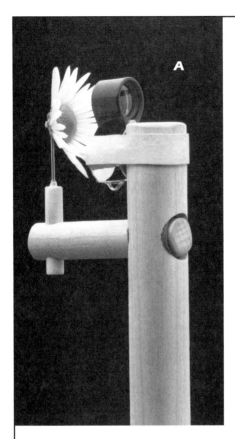

FIGURE 18A
How to Use Your
Homemade Microscope

(A) Use the eye of the canvas needle to examine liquids such as pond or gutter water. (B) Reverse the canvas needle in the needle holder to "spear" objects for closer examination. CAUTION: Needle points are extremely sharp. Always place the point of the needle into the hole in the dowel when not in use.

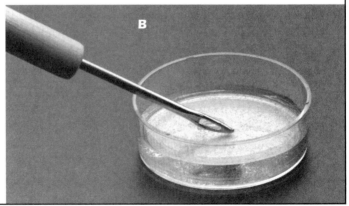

You can adapt the microscope to hold other objects (flowers, insects, etc.) by using the sharp point of the needle. Simply reverse the needle in the hole of the 1/4-inch dowel. See Figure 18.

MICROTECHNIQUES
When working with microscopes, the following techniques are especially useful.

Wet Mount
The most versatile technique in microscopy is the wet mount. It will allow you to observe microlife under the microscope. Place a drop of water to be examined in the center of a glass microscope slide, and then gently lower a coverslip (at a 45-degree angle) onto the drop.

Hanging-Drop Preparation
This is a drop of water that hangs vertically from the coverslip and allows you to view microlife forms enclosed inside it. The technique is useful in observing motile microlife forms. Use Figure 19 as a guide.

You will need a glass concavity slide, coverslip, a toothpick, petroleum jelly, and tweezers. Use the toothpick to apply a thin layer of jelly around the cavity of the glass slide. Place the drop of water to be examined in the middle of the coverslip (Figure 19A). Use the tweezers to quickly invert the coverslip so that the drop hangs (Figure 19B). Place the coverslip, with the hanging drop, over the cavity in the slide and gently press the coverslip to make a seal with the jelly (Figure 19C).

Dark-Field Microscopy
This allows you to easily view transparent and minute microlife forms, particularly hanging-drop preparations.

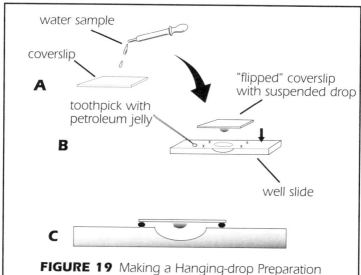

water sample

coverslip

A

toothpick with
petroleum jelly

B

"flipped" coverslip
with suspended drop

well slide

C

FIGURE 19 Making a Hanging-drop Preparation
(A) Hold a coverslip between your index finger and thumb.
Add a single drop of sample to the center of the coverslip.
(B) Carefully "flip" over the coverslip so that the drop "hangs."
Gently lower the coverslip onto the well slide that has been
prepared with four small dabs (x) of petroleum jelly.

A special dark-field light stop is used to create a black background for high-contrast views of the brightly lit subject.

Dark-field illumination requires a compound microscope with a condenser and filter holder. Use Figure 20 as a guide for converting your bright-field microscope to dark-field. The light stop—a small, circular, black paper disc—can be glued to the center of a clear plastic (acetate) disk that has been cut to fit the filter holder.

Turn on your light source and place a wet mount or hanging-drop preparation on the stage. Open the iris diaphragm. As you look through the eyepiece, focus the condenser until you see the best dark-field view. See the results in Figure 20.

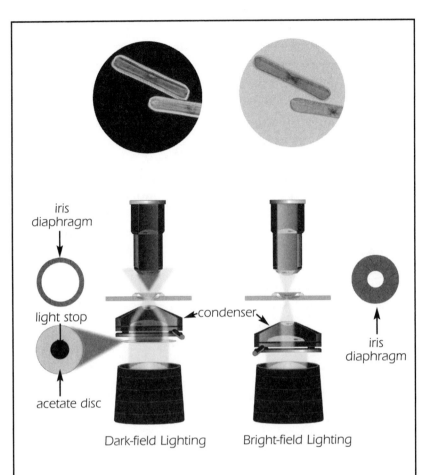

iris
diaphragm

light stop

condenser

iris
diaphragm

acetate disc

Dark-field Lighting   Bright-field Lighting

FIGURE 20 Dark-field Lighting
Dark-field lighting is useful for obtaining the greatest level of image contrast. This is done by brightly illuminating the object while creating a black background that makes it easier to observe internal detail. Use this technique in combination with the hanging-drop (an upside-down drop viewed from above) preparation provides for dramatic contrast views. A round dark-field light stop, made from black construction paper, is mounted on a clear, round, acetate disc that is cut to fit the filter holder under the condenser, is used to create a black background that better shows off the intricate detail of these diatoms.

OUT OF THE OOZE

Early micronaturalists spent hours peering into single-lens microscopes, observing microlife in mud oozes, puddles, gutter sediments and water, and other familiar locales. They then chronicled the changes they observed over time. For example, some micronaturalists observed that in winter or during dry periods, many protists formed protective coverings called *cysts*.

Begin investigating by preparing your own protist cultures. Collect mud, dried grass clippings, gutter water and sediments, decaying leaves, and so on; put them into jars, and then fill the jars about two-thirds full of bottled water. Let the jars stand for several days in indirect sunlight.

Periodically remove water from the jars using an eyedropper, make wet mounts, and observe under the microscope. Use identification guides to try to identify what you see. Take careful notes on what you observe. Over time, try to follow the same organisms from the same parts of the jars. Try to identify the feeding strategies of different protists. For instance, where do the scavengers or the hunter-killers congregate in the jar? Design experiments to test for sensitivity to temperature, pH, light, gravity, magnetism, sound, movement, and other stimuli.

SIZING UP MICROLIFE

You can estimate the size of a microlife form by comparing it with the size of the circular field of view in the microscope. To determine the diameter of the field, place a transparent plastic ruler (or a piece of millimeter-ruled graph paper) on the microscope stage. Use the low-power objective (4X or 10X) to obtain a clear image of the divisions of the ruler or rules on the graph paper. The distance between the ruled lines is the distance of the field of view at a particular magnification.

Generally, at 40X magnification, the field of view measures 4,000 µm; at 100X, the field measures 1,600 µm; at 430X, the field measures 375 µm. If an organism is half as long as the diameter of the low-power (100X) field, it measures approximately 800 µm.

MAKING MICROLIFE TRAPS

Nothing is certain—except change. Scientists studying the natural world use the term *succession* when they talk about change. Succession is the progressive replacement of one group of microlife (or any life-form) by another until a relatively stable microcommunity results. For example, suppose you placed 15 millileters (1 tbsp) of dried pond mud in a glass of bottled water. After all the sediment settled out, the first life-forms you would observe under the microscope probably would be bacteria. In a few days, you would observe small ciliates, which emerged from protective cysts, darting around and grazing on the bacteria. Still days (and weeks) later, a careful look into the microscope would reveal rotifers and other microcrustaceans grazing on the ciliates—a micro food chain! Use Figure 2 and Figure 40 to help you identify microlife forms[6].

An easy way to sample microlife populations is to set up traps that can easily be collected. Microlife will colonize (establish a home in or on) almost any type of

---

6 An excellent tool for microlife identification is *Guide to Microlife*. See the Appendix.

artificial material surface, such as polyurethane foam sponges, glass slides, pieces of plastic, or aquarium netting placed into quiet waters, moist sands, or soils.

You might want to set plastic traps in open waters (flat plastic pieces or sponges) attached to clothespins and set these traps at incremental distances along a rope or chain. This string of traps can be set either vertically or horizontally by attaching it to a series of floats.

Squeeze the contents from sponges left in the environment for several days (or even weeks) into a jar for study under the microscope. Return the traps to collect more microlife.

Use a flattened toothpick to scrape the collected biofilm (a thin layer of growing microlife forms that on a flat surface) from plastic pieces that have been suspended in water or immersed in mud or sand. Mix the scrapings with a drop of water on a clean microscope slide and observe under a microscope. If you want to stain these films, use Figure 3 as a guide.

- Do the kinds and numbers of colonizing microlife change from season to season? In the spring? Do they change following a sudden influx of fertilizer runoff?
- Use the diversity calculation in Chapter 6 to quantify your biological succession observations. In this calculation you are comparing the number of *taxons* present at various times in the development of a biofilm. A taxon is an individual of a certain type. You need to know not what each organism is, but only that each taxon has identical individuals. You would expect that a newly colonized substrate would have a low diversity index (i.e., a small number of taxons). A substrate that has been exposed to colonizers for a long

period of time would be expected to have a high diversity index (i.e., a large number of taxons).

- Biofilms are diverse (i.e., stable) microhabitats that are used to improve water quality. You can observe a biofilm in an aquarium filter. Remove portions of an external aquarium filter for study. Place small samples of biofilm material in a drop of water under the microscope. Add a coverslip and examine under both low power (100X) and high power (430X) of a compound microscope. Compare diversity indexes for various filter-material substrates over various time periods. Can you design an efficient colonizing medium that could be used to improve water quality in an aquarium?
- Research biofilms on the Web. Find out more about how biofilms are used to improve water quality.
- If possible, visit a sewage treatment plant. Ask for a sample of biofilm substrate (an inert material) from a trickle filter (like an aquarium filter) or for the scrapings from one. Keep these films moist until you can examine them under a microscope. Compare the diversity (see Chapter 6) and types of microlife forms found on the trickle filter with biofilms taken from riffle areas of streams. If you can't get to a sewage treatment plant, use an aquarium filter instead.

CHAPTER 5

PLANTS—
THE WORLD
OF GREEN

From moss to towering redwoods, plants lend a refreshing green to much of Earth. They are the silent factories that transform the sun's energy, providing oxygen and food through a remarkable chemical process called photosynthesis.

All plants have a multitude of microscopic sacs containing the chemical chlorophyll inside their cells. It is chlorophyll—a substance that just happens to be green—that powers photosynthesis.

Plants are nature's pharmacy, having evolved hundreds of complex chemicals that play vital roles in their lives and in ours. Some plants are natural insecticides, and many are used as spices, cloth dyes, and medicines.

About half a million plants are known, and most are adapted to life on land. The plant kingdom includes all the familiar plants: mosses, ferns, shrubs, trees, vines, and herbaceous plants.

TESTING FOR PHOTOSYNTHESIS

Plants usually produce more sugars by photosynthesis than they can use. They convert this excess sugar to starch for long- and short-term storage. Plants store starch molecules in clusters or grains. Some plants, such as potatoes, store starch in modified underground stems called *tubers*. Others, such as bananas, store starch in their fruit or in their seeds, as in the case of the corn plant.

Since iodine applied to starch turns starch granules a deep blue-black, you can use it to find out whether a known plant has just been photosynthesizing, where it stores its food, or whether an unknown organism is a plant.

To apply the starch test, you need to remove the green chlorophyll pigment that masks the starch. The chlorophyll molecule is present in an overwhelming amount and must be removed to observe the remaining starch molecules in the chemical test. Boil the leaves (or other plant parts) for 5 minutes and place the boiled parts in a sealed container of rubbing alcohol for a day or so. *Caution: Rubbing alcohol is a flammable liquid.* Then transfer the plant parts to a tray containing Betadine, an iodine product available in drugstores.

Caution: Be sure to wear goggles. Iodine is poisonous, so be careful to avoid ingesting or splashing your eyes with the Betadine.

To observe what color the chemical reaction of iodine and starch will look like, first try applying a drop of iodine to powdered starch. Mix a pinch of dry starch with a drop of iodine on a microscope slide. You should see a dark blue-black.

Allow this iodine-containing solution to react with the boiled leaves for 15 to 20 minutes. Gently wash off the iodine solution and inspect for the presence of starch. Then do the following:

- Test leaves from trees, ferns, flowers, lichens, grasses, freshwater plants, and so on. Test leaves at various times of the day and night to see if you can detect different dark brownish patterns indicating the presence of starch. Draw the patterns you observe. Does growing the plant in total darkness for three or four days make any difference? Test leaves that have mixed colors (like geraniums) and test flowers (botanists call them "modified leaves"). Make predictions about starch content before you do your testing. Are your predictions correct?
- Test roots and green stems. To prepare them, carefully use a single-edge razor blade or a potato peeler to make shavings of various plant roots or stems.
- Try testing different vegetables and fruits.
- The starch grains from various plant sources have different appearances. You can examine starch grain types by collecting a small amount of starchy material on a toothpick and mixing it in a drop of water on a clean glass slide. Add a coverslip and observe at 40X magnification.

    Most starch grains have a dark area called a *hilium*. This is the oldest part of the starch grain, around which additional starch is laid down over time.
- Collect samples from various plants (potatoes) or products (dry fabric starches) to examine and illustrate. For example, a starch grain type having a round-centered helium is manioc or tapioca. Manioc is a South American tropical plant that was one of the first plants domesticated in the Western hemisphere. Tapioca is used in laundry starches and fabric sizings as well as in the manufacture of explosives and glues.
- Research why starch is responsible for the "denting" of corn kernels, giving it the name "dent" corn.

PLANT HOMES

Take field trips to various habitats and note how plants attract or are used by other creatures. Keep a habitat diary. Record what types of life-forms use different plants. Use photographs to illustrate your finds.

A CLOSER LOOK AT ONE OF THE LARGEST OF PLANT CELLS

Some of the largest plant cells known are those comprising stamen hairs in spiderwort plants. Purchase a spiderwort plant in flower from a local florist or commercial grower. Use your magnifying glass to observe stamen hairs (see Figure 21). Pluck a stamen hair from a flower and observe a single cell through your lens. Each single bead is an individual plant cell. You will be able to see the cell nucleus if you view a wet mount under a compound microscope and observe at 100X.

WORLD'S LARGEST ORGANISM?

According to University of Colorado scientist Dr. Jeffrey Milton, a 43-hectare (106-acre) stand of genetically identical quaking aspens located in the Wasatch Mountains of south-central Utah is the world's largest organism. This stand of aspen is a clone (a lineage of genetically identical individuals), or *ramet*—each tree (clone) shares the same root system.

- Look at photographs of autumn aspens in travel guides. See whether you can pick out yellow aspen stands that look like circles on the mountainsides, with the tallest ramets in the center and the shorter ones at the perimeter.

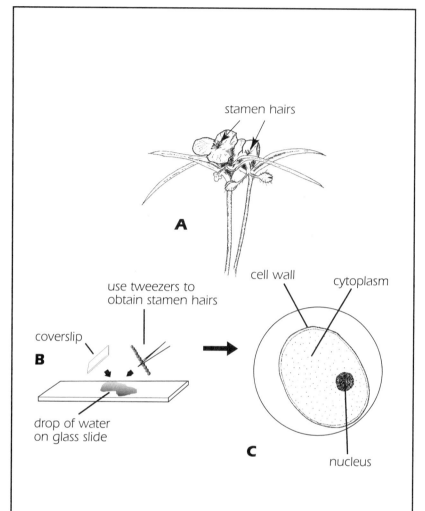

FIGURE 21 Studying Stamen Hair Cells
(A) Use forceps to remove a stamen hair from a spiderwort plant that is in flower. Note that the larger cells are nearest the base of the flower. (B) Make a wet mount preparation by placing a stamen hair in 1 or 2 drops of water on a microscope slide. Add a coverslip. (C) View at 40X magnification.

- If all the clones share a single root system, do you suppose that these special groups of aspens change color in the fall at the same time?

SURVEYING PLANTS

- Use field guides (see http://www.enature.com for plant identification guides) to identify as many plant types as possible. Keep a notebook of your observations, along with drawings and habitat descriptions. Try to learn what environmental and physical factors influence plant type and design. For example, why are ferns not found in deserts and cacti not found in swamps? What special structural features allow cacti to prosper in dry climates?
- Make a permanent reference collection of plants from a given habitat. Be sure to gather specimens only where collecting is permitted, and never take exotic or rare plants. Dig up the entire plant, roots and all. When a plant is too big, take a small piece of bark and a twig with leaves. Place collected plants in a plastic bag to keep them fresh until you get home.

  To preserve your plants, you will need a plant press. Use Figure 22 as a guide for making your own.

1. Bore about 20 holes in two pieces of 12 × 18 × 1/4-inch plywood or use two pieces of Peg-Board (Figure 22A).
2. Place plants between sheets of newspaper. Layer plant "sandwiches" with corrugated cardboard, and place them between plywood covers (Figure 22B). Use straps made of rope to squeeze plants (Figure 22C).

Mount dried, pressed plants to heavy white sheets of paper (30 × 45 cm [12 × 18 in.]) using small paper

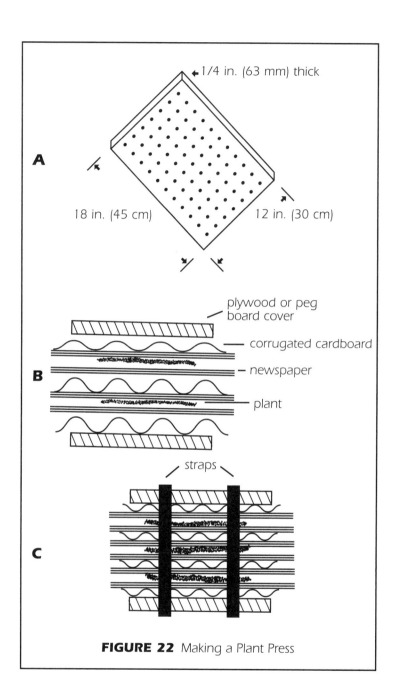

A

1/4 in. (63 mm) thick

18 in. (45 cm)   12 in. (30 cm)

B

plywood or peg board cover

corrugated cardboard

newspaper

plant

C

straps

FIGURE 22 Making a Plant Press

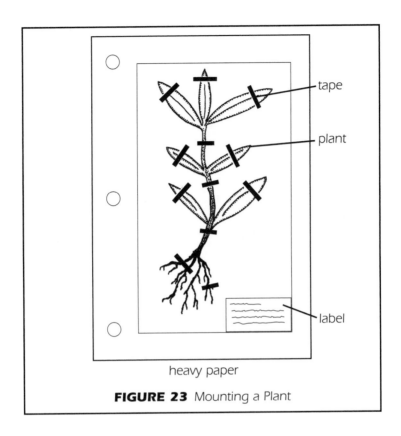

tape

plant

label

heavy paper

FIGURE 23 Mounting a Plant

strips glued at each end. Figure 23 shows a whole mounted plant. Label each sheet with the common and scientific names, date and place collected, your name, and the common features that place it in a particular group. Field guides will help you. Store your sheets flat in a cabinet or file box. Mothballs will help keep away insect pests that can damage your collection.

- Visit areas recently cleared of vegetation. Record which plants are initial colonizers. How did those plants get there? What adapts them to this role?

PLANT DISEASES

Soots, mildews, rots, galls, and a host of other names describe plant maladies. Use popular garden books to identify diseases on plants near where you live. With your parents' permission, try to treat the disease(s) you find. Write a report chronicling how your treatment(s) fared.

ROOTS

Roots anchor a plant and absorb water and nutrients from the soil. Some roots also store food. Use the starch test to identify plants that have storage roots.

- What kinds of plants in your area have the largest roots? The most intricate root systems? Dig up weeds and grasses. Erosion may have exposed the roots of other plants. If you live near a stream, river, or pond, identify the plants living near or in the water. Research plants that like water. They are called *hydrophytes*, or water-loving plants. Are their root systems different from those of plants that grow only on land?
- Consider plants that live in deserts and in tropical rain forests. Which plants would you expect to have the deepest or most widely spread root systems? Do some reading to check your answers. Perhaps what you learn will stimulate you to think of a project, even if you can't make a field trip on your own.

STEMS

The plant stem not only holds up leaves and flowers but provides a vital transport system through which water and mineral nutrients move from roots to leaves, while food (sugar) moves to the roots for storage.

- All stems have buds. A bud is a miniature shoot (a structure that has a small stem and tiny leaves). Look for other examples. Which is a stem—a potato or a sweet potato?
- In winter, go out and collect twigs. Dry them out and use field guides to identify them. Label identified winter twigs by tying tags to them that list the common and scientific names and the date and place collected.
- In most plants, water travels through tiny tubes that make up the *xylem*. A xylem is an internal water-conducting system in plants, made up of a series of tiny, often microscopic tubes that run lengthwise up the stem or trunk and into the roots, stems, and leaves. Xylem in celery can be made visible by immersing a stalk into water colored by food coloring. After a few minutes, remove the stalk and observe the plant's tiny water pipes by slicing across the stalk at various points along its length to trace tube bundles.

Investigate xylem further with these experiments.

- Obtain some freshly cut white carnation flowers. Establish two study groups: one group with its stems recut at an angle about 2 to 3 centimeters (1 in.) from the end, and the other not recut. Place both groups in vases containing water colored with food coloring. Time the passage of the colored water up the stems and to the flowers. Which study group has the faster water movement and the more intense flower coloring?
- Investigate the effect of water temperature on the rate of dye movement—how fast colored dye moves up the stem during a specific time period.
- The "wood" of most plants is made almost entirely of

xylem. Xylem provides support so that woody plants can grow to great heights. Other nonwoody, or herbaceous, plants rely on internal water pressure (*turgor*) to provide support. You can investigate this internal cell pressure using a dandelion stem. Dandelions and other "stem succulents" store water in cells lining the inside of the stem. Find a dandelion blossom and pick it. Slit the stem lengthwise into four or more "strips." Immerse these strips in a glass of water and watch what happens. Can you explain what is occurring?

- Research cycads, primitive plants whose ancestors shared the early Earth with dinosaurs. These plants have a unique ability to contract their trunks and roots to protect them against adverse environments. Find out how they do this.
- Do all stems carry out photosynthesis? What do you suppose is an easy test to find out?

LEAVES

Leaves are the major photosynthesizing sites of plants. They have highly modified structures, and their shapes and arrangements are important clues in identifying plants.

- Start a leaf collection and organize it by leaf shape and arrangement. Use field guides to help in identifying leaf types (see http://www.enature.com for an electronic field guide to leaves).
- From your collection of leaves, what do you conclude is the best structural design to maximize photosynthesis? For example, do grasslike leaves have the same area (length × width) as shrub or tree leaves? Is leaf area a good measuring tool, or are there others, like

the way leaves are positioned on the plant itself exposed and to sunlight?
- Observe the arrangement of leaves on any plant. What do you conclude about their placement on the stem?
- Notice how different plant leaves repel water. Do certain leaves have fuzz (tiny hairs) on the tops of their leaves? Are leaf surfaces waxy or sculptured to funnel water to or away from the plant? Use a spray bottle to mist leaves and observe the water droplets. How is leaf design important to a plant?

WHAT'S THE PH?

Acidity is expressed by pH, which is a logarithmic number. A one-unit change in pH is actually a tenfold change in acidity—the concentration of hydrogen ions (H^+) in a solution. For example, pure distilled water has a pH of 7.0—this value, in the middle of a scale that runs from 0 to 14 pH units, is termed *neutrality*. Thus a solution that has a pH of 6.0 is 10 times more acidic (i.e., 10 times more H^+) than pure distilled water. A solution whose pH is 5.0 is 100 times more acidic than pure water.

MAKING YOUR OWN PH PAPER

The pH can be determined by the use of indicators—substances that change color in response to various pH conditions. Litmus (a blue powder extracted from lichens) is a reagent commonly used in making litmus paper, which is used to determine pH. You can make your own indicator paper using other plant pigments (anthocyanins) whose colors range from rich reds to dark blues, depending upon the acidity of the solution.

What You Need

Knife and chopping board

Red cabbage

Saucepan

Strainer

Mason jar and lid

Sheets of 100% rag paper[7] (quality writing paper)

Clothespins and suspended clothesline

What To Do

1. Under adult supervision, chop the cabbage into small pieces and place in a saucepan. Cover the cabbage with water. Heat until it almost boils, stirring the liquid until a deep red color is obtained. Allow to cool.

2. Carefully pour the mixture through a strainer into a mason jar to separate the cabbage pieces from the liquid anthocyanin extract. Discard the cabbage.

3. Cut 100 percent rag paper into 2.5 × 20-centimeter (1 × 8-in.) strips. Immerse paper strips into the anthocyanin extract and then remove, hang with clothespins, and allow to dry. The anthocyanin molecule is a chemical indicator—a substance that displays a different color depending upon the acidity or alkalinity of the chemical environment. The ability to change the color of certain chemicals is one property used to classify substances as "acids" or

---

7 Look in stationary stores for fine-quality writing paper labeled "100% rag," which is made out of cotton, not cellulose fiber.

"bases." An *acid* is any compound that increases the number of hydrogen (H⁺) ions when dissolved in water. A *base* is any compound that increases the number of hydroxide (OH⁻) ions when dissolved in water.

pH PROJECTS

Caution: Put on protective eyewear.

- Dissolve a few grains of baking soda into water in a plastic bottle cap. Pour small amounts of the following materials into separate plastic bottle caps: white vinegar, lemon juice, tap water, milk of magnesia (solution of magnesium hydroxide), and household ammonia.
- In your notebook, create a data table that lists the known pH values of these solutions.

PH Data Table		
Substance	**pH**	**Anthocyanin Paper Color**
lemon juice	2.4	
vinegar	3.0	
pure water	7.0	
milk of magnesia	10.0	
ammonia	11.0	

- "Calibrate" your anthocyanin paper by dipping small pieces of it in each of the prepared solutions. Observe the color change and glue a small piece of this reacted paper to your notebook table on the row next to its reacted solution. This will provide you with a comparison standard to measure the pH of other "unknown" materials by observing the change in color of the anthocyanin paper.

- Test "unknowns" such as grapefruit juice, shampoos, and meat tenderizer solutions.
- Create another pH test-paper type using grape juice as the indicator.
- Compare your anthocyanin-extract indicator with litmus paper by repeating the above investigation. Do you obtain the same color data?

OTHER pH PROJECTS
- Use your anthocyanin-extract indicator paper to test other common substances around the home, including rain and melted snow.
- Research other plant materials such as turnips, beets, rose petals, and others for the presence of anthocyanins.

USING PLANTS TO FORECAST THE WEATHER
Test these plant signs.

Impending thunderstorm	Upturned leaves of silver maple trees
	Dandelions folded inward
Rain	Dry grass in morning
Nice day	Dew on grass in morning

Can you find other signs?

URBAN BOTANY
Conduct a plant inventory within a city block in three different locations: residential, commercial, and industrial.

Focus your attention on wild, not ornamental, plants. What plants are common to each habitat? How do they adapt? Which habitat is more diverse (has the largest number of different plants)? Conduct a diversity analysis (see Chapter 6) to find out which habitat is more diverse. Collect and preserve interesting plant forms.

- Why do sidewalk trees have rings of soil around them? Design an experiment that uses seedlings as stand-ins (substitutes) for the bigger trees.

NEWTON'S APPLE

Does light affect plants in ways other than in photosynthesis?

Caution: Put on protective eyewear.

- Find out whether light affects color change when some apples ripen from green to yellow or red. Sterilize three to six apples for 2 minutes in a 5 percent bleach solution (1 part bleach mixed with 19 parts water) to prevent spoilage.

Caution: Handle the bleach carefully.

Wrap the apples in
- black paper
- clear cellophane
- colored cellophane
- black paper with little windows made of clear and colored cellophane

Expose the apples to light for several days. What do you find? Try this experiment with both ripe and unripe red apples (if available), as well as green and yellow apples. Experiment, too, with changing colors of cellophane on one apple, as well as with different types of light—sunlight, tungsten, and fluorescent.

- Experiment with other fruits and vegetables to determine whether light affects color or ripening. Try pears, tomatoes, oranges, and beans.
- Does light affect growth of vegetables such as potatoes, carrots, and beets? To find out you will need a garden or good planters. As soon as the young plants emerge, spread different-colored plastic sheet material over plant rows. Make up a couple of hypotheses as to what will happen. After the growing season, harvest the plants and note the results. Were your guesses right?

FRUIT RIPENING AND PLANT HORMONES

Hormones are chemicals produced by living things that stimulate cellular changes. When fruit ripens, the flow of nutrients from a plant to its fruit is gradually stopped and its green skin pigment, chlorophyll, gradually disappears and is replaced by other pigments, which have been there all the time but not in as a high a concentration as chlorophyll. Other chemical changes occur in the flesh of fruit as well: Starch changes to sugar; pectin (a carbohydrate found in unripe fruit) breaks down, losing its stiffness; and the flesh softens.

Ripening fruit "breathes"—it takes in oxygen and gives off carbon dioxide. Oxygen is essential for the chemical reactions that occur during ripening. In addition, ripening also gives off another gas called *ethylene* (C_2H_4). Ethylene is produced by a chemical reaction involving *enzymes*. An enzyme is a chemical molecule; a protein that promotes a specific biochemical reaction. High temperatures inhibit enzymes.

Is fruit ripening a contained system, or is it affected by the environment? Let's use bananas for some experiments.

- In which circumstance does ripening occur faster if two equally green banana plants are compared—with one green banana placed in a sealed brown paper bag and the other left out on the kitchen counter? Hint: Sealing the bag increases C_2H_4 content.
- Is ripening time increased if two bananas—one green and the other ripe—are placed in a sealed brown paper bag?
- Does the container itself affect the rate of ripening? Try other packaging materials such as plastic or aluminum foil.
- Try wrapping a ripe banana in clear plastic wrap and then placing it along with a green banana in a brown paper bag. Does ripening of the green banana occur as quickly as when the ripened banana was unwrapped? Do other ripened fruits, like tomatoes or pears, demonstrate the same result?

Based upon your experiments, is ethylene a hormone? Is packaging green fruits in plastic wrap to ship them to market before they ripen a good idea?

Investigate what happens if you immerse an unripened tomato, while it is still on the vine, in very hot water for 5 minutes to deactivate the ethylene-producing enzyme. Will the treated fruit ripen?

Investigate if cold temperatures (or even freezing) affect fruit ripening. What do you suppose the effect of high levels of carbon dioxide have on fruit ripening? You could try an experiment in which unripened fruit is placed in plastic bags containing a piece of dry ice. Make sure that you also use a control in the experiment—i.e., an unripened piece of fruit in a similar plastic bag at the same temperature without the addition of dry ice.

Research on the Web how producers of fruits and vegetable on the West Coast send their products to markets on the East Coast.

WEED CONTROL WITHOUT CHEMICALS

Is mowing the lawn the best way to control weeds? Design an experiment to answer this question, but be sure to get your parents' permission before you begin. Hint: Try varying the depth of the cut or even leaving an area of the lawn uncut.

WHO'S BEEN VISITING THIS FLOWER?

Some plants have flowers that are shaped and positioned to attract the same pollinators (insects or mammals) or take advantage of the wind. This helps ensure that pollen is transferred to a given flower of the same species.

For example, honeybees are attracted to flowers that are blue or yellow and have petals resembling landing platforms. The pansy is one example.

Make some observations of flowers. Note landing platforms, different odors (or no odor), night bloomers versus day bloomers, colors (or the lack thereof), shapes, and so on.

Try to observe the pollinators. Wrap red cellophane over a flashlight to observe night pollinators without disturbing them. Construct your own "key to pollinators" and use it to make some general predictions about pollinators and flowers.

TREE RINGS

Have you ever counted the number of rings in a tree? *Dendrochronology* is the science of determining tree age according to the number of rings in its trunk.

Because of seasonal variations in cell growth in the woody parts of trees, springwood can be recognized as concentric light rings and summerwood as concentric dark rings. One set of light and dark rings, therefore, represents one year of growth.

Figure 24 shows a slab of red pine that is twenty-five years old. Growth was rapid during the first few years, but slowed down between the fourth and seventh years, probably because less water (in the form of rainfall or snowmelt) was available for spring growth.

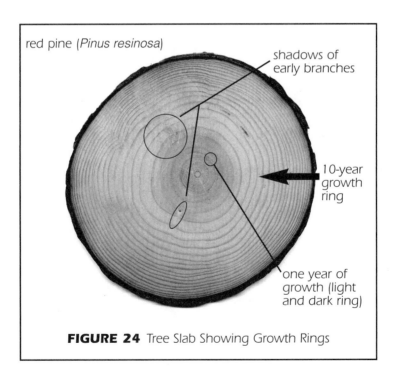

FIGURE 24 Tree Slab Showing Growth Rings

As the tree grew, crowding from nearby trees caused the rings to get progressively thinner. The shadowed areas indicating early branches can still be observed.

You can use this information to study tree growth near you. Try reading cut tree stumps or logs to reconstruct the age of the trees or the climate during the life of the trees. Check your findings against data from the weather bureau or from newspapers.

USING A PLANT THERMOMETER

Rhododendron (*Rhododendron maximum*) is an evergreen that retains its leaves throughout the year. These shrubs are adapted to protecting their broad leaves from bright sunlight and cold temperatures by darkening them and curling them up. Observe a sprig of leaves from this plant (or a potted plant) at various temperatures and times of the year. Compare the amount of leaf curl to air temperature readings. Use leaf curl to make a plant thermometer. How accurate is your plant thermometer? Illustrate your observations in your notebook; include drawings.

AUTUMN LEAVES

Chlorophyll is the main pigment in leaves. But for a leaf to stay green, chlorophyll must be synthesized constantly.

- What in the environment actually triggers the cessation of chlorophyll production—and thus the appearance of fall leaf colors? Is it something in the soil, the intensity of light, the length of the day or night, the temperature, the humidity, the amount or type of precipitation, or some other factor?
- Chart the color changes in the various trees and

shrubs where you live, beginning in September. Keep track of types of vegetation, area, weather, and so on. It's probably best to pick a small section to keep your statistics manageable.

- Why don't leaves all change to the same color? Why do some leaves on a tree not change color at all?
- Why do some trees change color faster than others?
- Find out whether a dry growing season causes premature coloration. You will need to research rainfall and color-display records in your area.
- Could mineral deficiencies affect coloration in houseplants or trees? Use a soil test kit to investigate this. You may be able to explain why one stand of trees in the park turns red and not another, or why one group of plants in your garden or indoor greenhouse is reddish. What minerals are involved, if any?
- Use masked plant pigments to create a photographic image. Use Figure 25 as a guide. Select a green fruit such as a tomato. Carefully wrap aluminum foil around the unripened fruit while it is still attached to the plant. After 7–10 days, carefully unwrap a portion of the foil, and tape (around the edges) a photographic negative securely onto the fruit's surface. Carefully add additional aluminum foil around the photographic negative so that you create a window. Wait another 10 days, pick the unripened fruit, and remove the negative. What do you observe? Write a report that explains your results. Can this experiment be done with large green leaves on a tree?

TROPISMS

Many plants actually move in response to certain environmental stimuli. Sensitivity to gravity is *gravitropism*; to

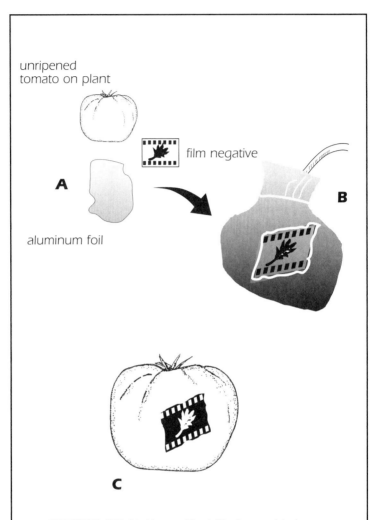

unripened
tomato on plant

film negative

A

B

aluminum foil

C

FIGURE 25 Making a Plant Photographic Image
(A) Wrap aluminum foil around a green (unripened) tomato
fruit while it is still on the plant. (B) Create a window on the
foil that fits the shape of a 35 mm negative frame. Use mask-
ing tape to secure the negative to the aluminum foil. (C) After
10 days, pick the fruit and remove the negative and aluminum foil. Can you observe a "photographic" image?

light, *phototropism*; to water, *hydrotropism*; and to touch, *haptotropism*.

- To investigate gravitropism, use four corn seeds soaked in water for one or two days. Carefully arrange them in the bottom of a mayonnaise jar so that they are in a circle, equidistant from one another, with their pointed ends facing inward. Use Figure 26 as a guide.
- Carefully place a thin layer of nonabsorbent cotton over the seeds. Fold white paper towels to the approximate size of the jar opening and push them down into the jar to secure the seeds and cotton in position. Wet the paper towels thoroughly and seal the jar with its cap. Place the jar on its side and look at the four corn seeds through the bottom of the jar. Rotate the jar so that one kernel is pointing straight up. Use bits of clay to hold the jar in that position. Make sure the jar is placed in dim light conditions. Observe your experiment over 5 to 7 days. Make notes and draw what you see. Do different parts of the plant react differently to gravity? Do the roots and shoots always grow from the same part of the seed? How long does a plant take to respond to gravity? Is it the same for all parts?
- Test potted plants (of the same type and height) for their response to gravity. Orient them in positions similar to those of the corn seeds—horizontal, vertical, and upside down. Place all plants in the dark. How do plants react to the effects of circular motion? Do they react the same way as they do to gravity?
- You can also use the Venus's-flytrap plant to investigate tropisms. Carefully investigate how the trap is sprung on mature plants. Do natural occurrences such

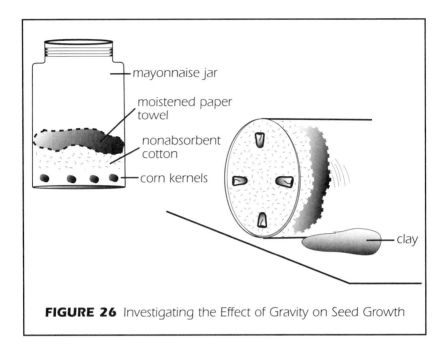

mayonnaise jar

moistened paper towel

nonabsorbent cotton

corn kernels

clay

FIGURE 26 Investigating the Effect of Gravity on Seed Growth

as raindrops spring the trap? Do soil conditions affect the trap mechanism?

- Observe ivy and other vines for their response to touch. How do the growing tendrils react when they come into contact with solid objects? What happens if the tendrils are cut off?

- Hydrotropism can be observed when ground moisture is low. Construct a root observation "jug" to observe this response. Use Figure 27 as a guide. Place dry and moist soil in the root observation container, as shown. Then plant five corn seeds along the flat face about 2 to 3 centimeters (1 in.) deep. Cover the soil with mulch or grass clippings to hold in soil moisture. Draw what you observe over a two- to three-week period. Do plant roots respond to soil moisture?

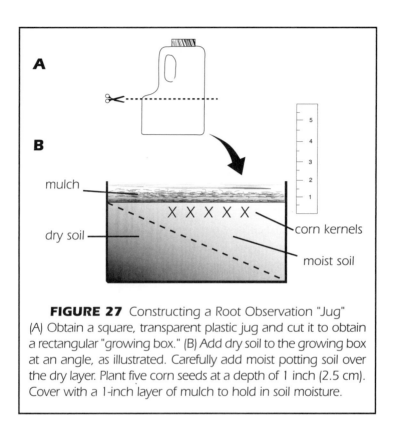

FIGURE 27 Constructing a Root Observation "Jug" (A) Obtain a square, transparent plastic jug and cut it to obtain a rectangular "growing box." (B) Add dry soil to the growing box at an angle, as illustrated. Carefully add moist potting soil over the dry layer. Plant five corn seeds at a depth of 1 inch (2.5 cm). Cover with a 1-inch layer of mulch to hold in soil moisture.

If so, how? Do they seem to "search" for soil moisture? Try different types of soils—for example, clay, sand, and potting soil—and observe their moisture-holding capacities. Is a drenching rain more beneficial than a light, steady shower?

PLANTS WITH AN APPETITE!

Of the world's 500 known types of carnivorous plants, only a few are found in the United States. It is best to purchase these from specialized growers or from biological supply companies instead of trying to locate them in the wild. As a group, they are remarkable organisms.

- Whatever plant you study (Venus's-flytrap, pitcher plant, or sundew), read about it and try to discern the strategy it uses to attract its catch.
- Use a video camera with slow-motion capability to study these plants.
- Some insects (such as ants) produce chemicals that are a defense against animal predators. Are these chemicals successful against carnivorous plants?
- Do these plants literally digest their meals (produce acids and digestive juices) or do they "eat" their meals another way? You will need a microscope to determine that.

PEST-AWAY
Test these natural plant-control measures for their effectiveness as insect repellers.

ants	boiled and cooled extract of elder leaves poured over a nest
	marigolds planted near a nest
aphids	boiled extract of rhubarb sprayed on stems and leaves
slugs	thyme (an herb) planted in a garden or applied in dried form
moths	dry thyme and sage (herbs) in cloth packets
flies	dried elder leaves in a basket on a table

SEEDS—CAPSULES OF LIFE
Most plants reproduce by producing seeds. The plants' survival depends on their ability to reproduce. That, in turn, depends on the mechanisms they use to disperse

seeds. In flowering plants, seeds are protected by a structure called the fruit. In *gymnosperms* (pines and spruces), seeds are protected by cones. Ferns use spores to disperse themselves. (Look at the underside of fern leaves to observe spore packets.)

- Read more about seeds and fruits. Dry fruits, like green pea pods, do not contain the pulpy, fleshy material that characterizes fleshy fruits, such as apples. Make a collection of seeds and fruits and record the fruit type, number of seeds, plant adaptations, and observed method of seed dispersal. Make a drawing of each seed you find. Use reference books to help identify plants and their seeds.
- Flight-test some of your collected seeds. Release each seed from a height and record how long it stays aloft and how far it travels. Do this on both windy and calm days. Diagram the flight path of each seed. Try counting the number of hairs on a dandelion seed. Is the number always the same? Try removing some hairs and see if the flight characteristics are the same.
- Make models of maple, ash, or tree of heaven seeds. Use cardboard and pennies (for the seed part). How large a model can you build? Can you improve on nature's design?
- Investigate seed structure by dissecting various seeds (such as dried beans). Sometimes it is helpful to soak the seeds in water for one or two days before dissecting. Use a drop of Betadine (available at drugstores) to test the seed for starch. Which structure does not stain?
- A seed planted and provided with the proper temperature, amount of oxygen, and moisture will usually germinate. Does storing seeds at freezing tempera-

tures or at very high temperatures 65° C (150° F) affect germination? What about alternating freezing and thawing? Will seeds germinate if placed between moist paper towels inside a sealed mayonnaise jar in which a small amount of steel wool and vinegar is placed to remove oxygen? Can you germinate seeds that are totally immersed in water?

IMPRESSIONS

In leaves, tiny pores called *stomata* allow the release of water vapor into the air, as well as the passage of gases (carbon dioxide and oxygen) into and out of the plant during photosynthesis.

You can make impressions of these outer leaf surfaces to visualize these tiny stomata by using Duco cement. Use a brush to apply a thin layer of cement to the leaf's surface (top or bottom). After the cement dries, use tweezers to carefully peel away the resultant film from the leaf. Use Figure 28 as a guide. Make permanent microscope slide preparations by placing the film on a microscope slide. Add one drop of corn syrup and cover with a coverslip. Examine your slide under a microscope at 100X.

- How many stomata does a leaf have in an area of 1square centimeter? Note: You could use a metric ruler to measure and mark a 1 square centimeter area to cast[8]. Is this number the same for a particular type of plant, or does it change?
- Are stomata more numerous on the bottom or top surfaces of leaves?

---

8 The area of the field of view at 40X magnification is 12.5 square millimeters (at 100X it is 2 square millimeters).

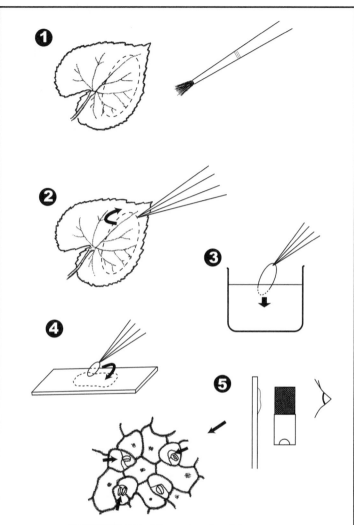

FIGURE 28 Observing Leaf Stomata
(1) Brush with Duco cement. (2) Pick up dried cement cast from leaf with tweezers. (3) Dip leaf cast into water. (4) Place leaf cast on microscope slide. (5) Observe stomate impressions (arrows) against a lit background under a microscope or with a magnifying glass.

- Could you use the number of stomata in leaves to identify different types of plants?
- Do desert plants like cacti have more stomata than do nondesert or tropical plants?
- Do plants keep stomata open longer in very wet conditions, or in periods of drought?
- When are stoma pores open on plant leaves? When they are closed? Relate your findings to the process of photosynthesis.

CHAPTER 6

INVERTEBRATES— ANIMALS WITHOUT BACKBONES

Animals inhabit nearly every place on Earth, from the bottoms of oceans to the tops of mountains. There are animals that crawl, swim, jump, and fly. There are large animals like elephants, and animals such as rotifers that are so small that you need a microscope to see them. Animals are the most diverse form of life on Earth. Recent estimates put the number of animal species at 100 million or more, and it may surprise you to know that most of these species are insects. (There is, by contrast, only one species of human!)

Despite the number of species, all animals can be (fairly) neatly divided into two main groups: those with an internal support structures (like bony skeletons) and those without them. You and your cat have bony skeletons, but your pet sea anemone and starfish don't.

For a variety of reasons, invertebrates make the best

subjects for animal projects. For one thing, there are more of them. They are also simpler than vertebrates. Observing or working with their cells, organs, or genetic material is easier.

LOOKING AT HYDRA AND OTHER MICROSCOPIC ORGANISMS

How do you know when something is an animal? All animals share several features. They are mobile; they have complex sensory organs; and they eat (take food into their bodies and incorporate its nutrients into body cells) in some fashion. In other words, animals that appear motionless can eventually be seen performing some type of movement. And organisms that move aren't necessarily animals unless they satisfy the other two requirements. For example, a Venus's-flytrap moves to catch its prey but, lacks complex sensory organs and doesn't really eat its food, even though it looks that way. (Venus's-flytraps and other carnivorous plants usually live in moist places where they get little or no nitrogen from the soil. They obtain nitrogen from the insects they trap—a sort of insect fertilizer.)

A good animal to begin experimenting with is the hydra. Hydras are soft, transparent animals that can stretch to nearly 1 to 2 centimeters (0.05 in.) when fully extended. Their tentacles make them appear to be frayed pieces of string. In nature, they live in ponds and streams, where they attach themselves to plant stems and the undersides of leaves. The most common types are brown hydras and green hydras.

To collect hydras, obtain a large quantity of water plants or fallen leaves from pools, shallow lakes, or slow-moving streams. Place a group of plants with pond water or stream water in a white tray and place the tray in a sunny (but not hot) indoor location. After about an hour, you should be able to observe hydras on the surface of the water and on the sides of the container. Use an eyedropper to transfer the hydras to a jar filled with pond water. If necessary, you can store the collected hydras in the refrigerator. Be sure to change the water weekly.

Observe the feeding habits of the hydras. Transfer some of the hydras to a new jar filled with pond water and feed them newly hatched brine shrimp, bits of your dinner, or fish food. Do the hydras respond differently to different types of food?

Carefully use a fine needle to stimulate various parts of a hydra. Do this before and after cooling the hydra in jars in the refrigerator for 2 or 3 hours. Does temperature affect what you see?

- Study the effects of over-the-counter drugs such as caffeine or aspirin on hydras. Dissolve a single aspirin or antidrowsiness tablet in 30 milliliters (1 oz.) of water. Construct a microaquarium using Figure 29 as a guide to observe hydras under various experimental conditions. In your notebook, record the dose of the drug you will be administering. For example, a 325-milligram tablet dissolved in 30 milliliters of water would have a concentration of about 11 milligrams per milliliter. Use an eyedropper to transfer some hydras to the microaquarium. Transfer them in as small a drop of pond water as possible. Then add a specific number of drops of your drug solution to fill up the microaquarium. For example, there are about 20 drops in 1 milliliter. So if it took 60 drops to fill the microaquarium, you added approximately 33 milligrams of the drug (minus the small volume in the transfer drop). Keep careful records of your calculations and transfer volumes. Watch what happens to

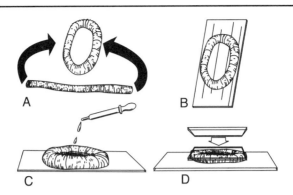

FIGURE 29 Constructing a Microaquarium
(A) Roll a piece of clay* into a 5-inch long tube on a flat surface using the palm of your hand. Form the tube into a circle. (B) Place the circle onto a clean microscope slide. Gently press down to assure a good seal. (C) Add sample. (D) Carefully add a coverslip.
* If possible, use silicone culture gum, an inexpensive material that allows oxygen to pass into the well's interior to prolong organism viability for days.

the hydras after their exposure to the drug(s). Do they contract or extend their bodies? Do they respond as quickly to a stimulus, like a fine needle? How are they at capturing food organisms like brine shrimp?

- Try different kinds of water in your microaquarium— tap water, tap water that has sat in a jar for several days, bottled water, and pond water. Do hydras respond differently? If so, why?
- Obtain (from a scientific supply company) or try to collect other organisms, such as *Daphnia*, rotifers, and *Planaria*. Try the same general types of experiments as you did with the hydras. When you are through with your experiments, return the hydras to where you found them.

INVERTEBRATES WITH CHEMICAL DEFENSES

Some invertebrates have nonlethal chemical defenses. Investigate the following organisms for chemical defenses: slugs, millipedes, and stinkbugs. Feed various insects to toads and frogs. What happens? Find out if other invertebrates use chemical defenses, such as making themselves wet or creating a foul odor.

HATCHES

Most invertebrates reproduce by laying eggs. The eggs incubate for a while and then hatch. A lot of interesting experiments can be done to learn more about hatching.

A good animal to work with at first is the brine shrimp. You can buy the eggs at pet stores. Follow the instructions on the cover for hatching and rearing brine shrimp; then strike out on your own.

Find out whether the number of brine shrimp that hatch from eggs are affected by water temperature if a consistent volume (1/4 teaspoon) of eggs are placed in saltwater to hatch. Can the eggs survive freezing and thawing before they are introduced to the water? Experiment with other variables during the hatching process, such as type of water (carbonated versus noncarbonated), salinity (more or less concentrated salt solution than recommended on the package), iodized versus uniodized salt in the water, oxygen content (using boiled saltwater that has been allowed to cool versus water that has not been boiled), acidity (adding drops of vinegar to increase acid conditions), and the presence of other nutrients such as fertilizer or dirt.

- Find other invertebrates to work with. Rotifers are also used as fish food, and pet stores usually have vials of dried *Branchionus* eggs for hatching. These fascinating microscopic creatures were first described by the famed micronaturalist Antonie van Leeuwenhoek in 1703. *Branchionus* range in size up to 300 µm— about 0.33 millimeter. You will need a microscope to view these rotifers.

Rotifers are cell-constant animals. This means that each individual in a species has exactly the same number of cells in its body. Of what use do you think rotifers could be to medical research?

THE LIFE STORY OF THE MOSQUITO AND OTHER MICRONATURALIST TALES

In the late 1600s, an Englishman named Robert Hooke made microscopes and used them to examine small objects. Hooke's work indicated the great potential of the microscope for biological investigation. Hooke introduced the world to the living cell, to microscopic fungi, and to the life story of the mosquito . . .

Of the Water-Infected Gnat
This little creature . . . was a small scaled or crufted Animal, which I have often observed to be generated in Rain-water. I have also observed it in Pond and River-water. It is supposed by some, to deduce its first original from the putrefaction of River-water, in which, if it have flood any time open to the air, you shall seldom miss, all the Summer long. . . .

Visit the website http://www.octavo.com to learn more about Hooke's microscopic discoveries and read printed materials and rare first editions of other great science books written by Sir Isaac Newton, Benjamin Franklin, and others.

CAUTION: MOLLUSKS AT REST

After insects, mollusks are the most diverse group of animals on Earth. Most mollusks have bodies that are covered by shells. Some typical mollusks are snails, slugs, clams, and oysters.

Since snails and slugs are so common throughout the United States, they are a good choice for projects. However, you may want to experiment with shellfish if you live near the ocean or an estuary. Shellfish (such as clams) can also be found in lakes and rivers.

Catching land snails and slugs is best done early in the morning, following a heavy rain, or in generally wet places. Look for snails and slugs in the woods or gardens and under leaves, stones, and rotting logs. If you live in a big city, check the parks, neighbors' gardens, window boxes, and so on. You may be able to buy snails at some markets. You can track these mollusks by following their silvery mucus trails.

You can collect pond snails from under pond weeds, floating plants, or submerged rocks. Saltwater snails and other mollusks can be found in tide-pool areas, but be sure not to collect in protected areas. For example, tide-pool collecting in many parts of California is generally against the law. (Of course, there's no law against touching and observing.)

Keep land snails and slugs in a sealed jar (with air holes) in the refrigerator (with your parents' permission). Keep aquatic snails in an aquarium or a jar with pond water.

- Crowd a bunch of snails (of either kind) together in a small space, like a plastic jar, so that they cannot move. (Be sure to punch air holes in the top, or the snails will die.) Put the jar in the refrigerator (with your parents' permission). What happens? Keep some snails this way for several days, others for a week or two, and, if you have the time, some for a month or more. At various times, remove some snails from the jar and let them gradually warm up, or place some of the snails in warm water for 10 to 60 minutes. What happens?

- Look for groups of snails or slugs in nature. Does their behavior resemble that of the snails or slugs in your "lab"? What do snails do during the winter? When it's dry? When there's snow? Do some research on estivation, which is a period of inactivity or dormancy during a drought. Do snails and slugs estivate and not hibernate? What about clams, mussels, and oysters? Do some reading about commercial shellfish harvesting or talk to fishermen. Does what you find or hear agree with what you have observed in your lab or in field investigations?

- Snails and slugs, of course, are famous for their slow pace. "Moving at a snail's pace" is one expression; "sluggish" is a word you probably have used or heard. Snails and slugs travel through the use of an appendage called a foot. Get a better view of how these mollusks use this appendage by placing a snail or slug on top of a pane of glass and viewing the foot from underneath using a magnifying glass. Use this glass pane observation method to measure a "snail's pace"—use a metric ruler and a glass-marking pencil to measure and mark distance on the glass, and then time how long it takes a particular mollusk to travel that distance.

- Design an experiment that measures a mollusk's response to various environments, both chemical and physical. Investigate chemical environments by placing a mollusk on paper towels dampened with vinegar (acidic environment) or a solution of baking soda (mix 5 milliliters [1 tsp.] in 30 milliliters [1 oz.] of water) (basic environment). Design an experiment that studies the effect of a rough surface, such as sandpaper, on mollusks. Will they avoid such surfaces?

- What do snails and slugs eat? Are they scavengers? How do they locate food? Do they smell it? Do they use their tentacles to help them locate food? How would you find out? Find out why snails bred to be eaten are often fed mulberry leaves. Investigate the eating habits of other mollusks. For example, how does the oyster eat?

EARTHWORMS: NATURE'S SUBTERRANEAN ENGINEERS

Charles Darwin, the biologist who formulated the theory of evolution, made detailed observations of earthworms for years and believed that they had some "degree of intelligence." He delighted in demonstrating earthworm behavior to houseguests. On his piano stood a row of flowerpots containing earthworms. At night, they would emerge to eat leaves. When certain low notes were played, the worms would retreat into their burrows.

Darwin reported that earthworms have food preferences. See if you can demonstrate this by building a worm box, adding soil and worms, and spreading different types of leaves on the surface. Also try fresh and dried grass clippings, flowers, and other plant parts. Investigate outdoor worms to see if they behave the same way in nature.

- Does sound or other vibrations affect your worms? Do your worms prefer loud or soft music? What good does it do to worms to be sensitive to vibrations—if indeed they are?

- Are worms sensitive to colors or intensities of light, amounts of moisture, temperatures, and surface textures? Experiment to see whether worms prefer one type of soil over another. If they do, can you isolate the "ingredient" responsible for the preference?

COLLECTING SOIL CRITTERS

A myriad of soil organisms can be observed by coaxing critters from the soil using a Berlese apparatus. You will need a 2 liter soda bottle, paper towels or a sponge, a small piece of insect screen, rubbing alcohol, and a gooseneck light (see Figure 30).

Cut off the top of the soda bottle. Place a moistened paper towel or sponge in the bottom of the bottle. Turn the top of the bottle upside down and place the screen into the spout.

To use the Berlese apparatus, place leaf litter and a small amount of the underlying soil and pinecones on the screen. Position the lamp 5 centimeters (2 in.) above the bottle, and turn on the light.

It may take a day or two for the light and heat from the bulb to drive the soil critters through the screen into the bottle. Experiment with soils, leaf litter, twigs, and cones from different habitats. Use guidebooks to identify what you find.

You can use this collecting technique in projects of your own design to investigate insect diversity, the effects of pesticides in certain areas, and the effects of pollution.

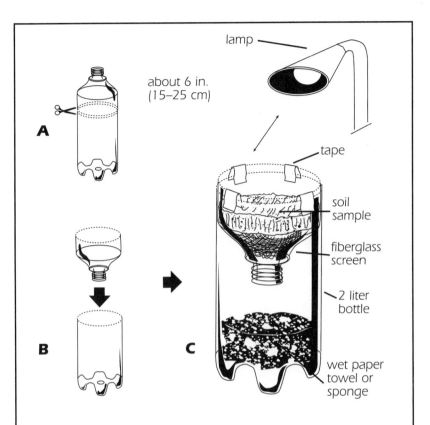

FIGURE 30 Berlese Funnel Apparatus
for Collecting Soil Critters

(1) Cut off the top of a 2 L soda bottle approximately 15–25 cm (6 in.) from the top (A). (2) Place a moistened paper towel or sponge in the bottom of the soda bottle. (3) Turn the top of the soda bottle upside down and place a piece of fiberglass window screen into it. (4) Place a couple of handfuls of soil or leaf litter on top of the fiberglass screen. Gently shake or tap the bottle top so that small, loose dirt particles fall through. (5) Insert the upside-down bottle top into the soda bottle bottom (B) and tape the two pieces together. (6) Place your Berlese apparatus underneath an incandescent light source (C) in an area where it will not be disturbed. Turn on the light bulb and leave the apparatus undisturbed for a day or so.

COMMUNITY MEETINGS: Studying Biodiversity Among Ecosystems

(For Advanced Young Scientists)

A *community* is all the populations of organisms that live and interact in the same place—an *ecosystem*—at a given time. Explore how environmental factors shape the *biodiversity*—the variety of life—in ground litter (accumulated organic material between the ground and root system of plants) ecosystems in the following project.

What You Need
Tape measure
4 pencils
Trowel
Plastic bags
Berlese apparatus (see Figure 30)
White or black construction paper
Magnifying glass or stereomicroscope
Camel-hair brush

What To Do

1. Locate two different ecosystems near where you live. Examples include a lawn litter ecosystem, forest litter ecosystem, bare ground ecosystem, a flower-bed litter ecosystem, or a sidewalk crack ecosystem.

2. Use the tape measure and pencils to establish a 15-centimeter (6-in.) square investigation area for each ecosystem (use a 60-centimeter [24-in] distance for the sidewalk crack ecosystem).

3. Use a trowel to collect litter material from the area

around each investigated ecosystem. Place collected material in two separate plastic bags.

4. Set up a Berlese apparatus (see Figure 30) for each ecosystem investigated.

5. Examine collected specimens from the different litters, placed on sheets of white or black construction paper, using a magnifying glass or stereomicroscope. Use a camel-hair brush to retrieve and manipulate delicate organisms for examination. It is not necessary to identify any collected organism. Simply group together like organisms, reported as taxons (taxonomic groups of any rank or size). You do not have to know what each organism is, only that each taxon contains identical individuals.

6. For each ecosystem studied, compile the number of taxons and number of organisms per taxon and record these data in your notebook.

7. Calculate the diversity index for each studied ecosystem using the following formula and hypothetical example.

$$\text{DIVERSITY} = \frac{N\,(N-1)}{\Sigma n\,(n-1)}$$

N = total number of individuals of all species
n = number of individuals of a species (taxon)
(Σ is a mathematical symbol meaning "the sum of sums")

Example:

ECOSYSTEM 1: *sidewalk crack*

Taxon 1   96
Taxon 2   4

$$\frac{100\,(100-1)}{96\,(96-1)+4\,(4-1)} = \frac{9900}{9132} = 1.08$$

ECOSYSTEM 2: *forest litter*

Taxon 1 20
Taxon 2 3
Taxon 3 30
Taxon 4 37
Taxon 5 10

$$\frac{100(100-1)}{20(20-1)+3(3-1)+30(30-1)+37(37-1)+10(10-1)} = \frac{9900}{2678} = 3.70$$

In this example, Ecosystem 2 (forest litter), with a diversity index of 3.70, is more diverse than Ecosystem 1 (sidewalk crack litter), which has a lower diversity index, 1.08.

Use your data to answer the following.

- Would the life-forms collected within one ecosystem survive in the other?
- Would a rain shower or other climatic condition or event impact each ecosystem differently?

THE PITFALL TRAP—ANOTHER COLLECTING TOOL

The pitfall trap is another useful tool for the naturalist. It is used in projects to study invertebrate diversity, population densities, and distribution, to compare samples from different habitats, to explore seasonal or daily animal activity patterns, and to detect the effects of pollution or acid rain.

To create a pitfall trap, bury a large can so that its rim is level with the ground surface. Put a small cup at the bottom of the can and a wide-mouth funnel on top of the cup. Fill the cup with 2.5 centimeters (1 in.) of rubbing alcohol to kill and preserve what falls into the trap (see Figure 31).

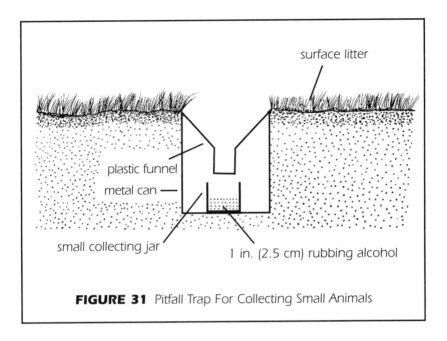

surface litter

plastic funnel

metal can —

small collecting jar

1 in. (2.5 cm) rubbing alcohol

FIGURE 31 Pitfall Trap For Collecting Small Animals

To get comparisons, place your traps in different locations at different times of the day or during different seasons.

A CLOSER LOOK AT INSECTS

- Investigate the effect of light of different intensities on insects. Investigate, too, the effect of colors, ultraviolet and infrared light, magnetic and electric fields, and two light beams set at a right angle. Work with insects in all stages of growth. Look for differences in responses at the different stages. For example, you might want to place a mealworm and a small amount of bran cereal bedding (or dampened paper towels) in a clear plastic box and observe the effect of placing a magnet or wrapped wire coil (creating an electromagnetic field) on the animal. Similarly, does exposing a ladybug beetle to the same conditions affect movement patterns? (Have the insect walk across an ink pad and then transfer the insect to the observation box and begin the experiment. The insect's tracks are your experimental record.)

- Do some reading on pheromones and insect communication. Find out which insects communicate using their sense of smell. (One insect group that does is ants.)

- If you aren't allergic to bee stings, investigate the feeding behavior of honeybees. Design experiments to determine whether bees can distinguish colors. How do they communicate? If you aren't sure whether you're allergic to bee stings, consult a knowledgeable adult before working around bees. You may be fortunate to live near apiculturists (beekeepers) who may allow you to observe bee communities. Sometimes local farm markets sell honey and have a beehive on the premises for patrons to observe.

- Fly fisherman tie artificial flies that they claim can fool trout. If you fish or know someone who does, do some checking to see if this is true. What seems to "fool" the fish—the way the lure looks or how it is manipulated in the water?

- Try to create nonchemical insecticides or insect repellents using different colors of light (colored filters do the trick), magnetic fields, sounds, smells, and food derivatives (such as lemon oil).

- Some scientists believe that ants (family Formicidae) contribute to the world's growing acid rain problem when they release formic acid when defending themselves, communicating with one another, and dying. Formic acid makes up most of the acid in acid rain.

Investigate the relationship between ants and acid rain. If such a relationship exists, how would you combat it without using insecticides or creating a pollution problem?

- Ants and other insects have special chemical receptors in their antennae that help them locate food. Find out if ants can tell the difference between soft drinks sweetened with sugar and with a sugar-free sweetener. On a concrete surface, such as a sidewalk, create two small pools of the same soft drink brand—one artificially sweetened, the other sweetened with sugar. Make sure that there is a 15- to 20-centimeter (6- to 8-in.) separation between the two pools. Are an ant's antennae receptors configured to sense sweetener molecules?
- Do research on aspartame. How does its molecular structure compare with sugar?
- See if an ant's receptors are sensitive to carbon dioxide gas. What happens if you breathe on a group of ants?

SUGARING

Here is an easy way to attract moths and other insects for study without using expensive blacklight traps. Mix sugar with a little honey until you have a thick mixture. Apply the mixture with a brush to tree trunks at dusk. Return with a collecting jar and flashlight to collect the baited insects.

Make a collection of insects captured this way. You may want to create a "general" collection that illustrates the major insect orders (see Insect Groups table on the next page) or conduct a diversity investigation (see Community Meetings in this chapter) to learn more about how insect populations change in various habitats such as in a backyard, around a pond, in a marsh, or in deep woods. For example, are odonates (dragonflies) more common in a marsh or pond habitat in a woodland park? Refer to some of the books on insects in the reading list at the end of the book, or go to http://www.enature.com to find an electronic field guide to insects.

Insect Groups	
Order	Examples
Odonata	dragonflies
Orthoptera	grasshoppers, crickets, mantids
Hemiptera	bugs
Lepidoptera	moths, butterflies
Coleoptera	beetles
Hymenoptera	wasps, bees
Diptera	flies

SUPER COOL INSECTS

Insects such as the gall moth (*Epiblema scudderiana*) spend the winter within spindle-shaped galls in the stems of goldenrod plants. These insects have evolved a strategy of freeze avoidance that utilizes the physics of *supercooling*. Part of this strategy is to void all gut (intestine) contents—eliminating any potential ice-starting *nucleators*—as well as accumulating high levels (as much as 19 percent of body weight) of an internally produced *cryoprotectant* (antifreeze).

- Use Figure 32 as a guide in locating moth galls on goldenrod stems in the fall or winter months. If possible, be especially observant as to the vertical position of the galls on stems. Are the observed galls always high enough on the stems to be continuously exposed to winter conditions and not covered by snow? Collect stem measurement data in your field notebook, possibly including some photographs, especially following a heavy snow. Take temperature measurements in the field—in the snowpack and next to the gall on the goldenrod plant. Is snow a good insulator and thus a threat to the insect in the gall?
- Collect galls for detailed examination at home. Use a sharp knife or single-edge razor blade to section the

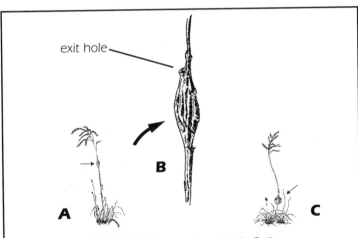

FIGURE 32 Locating Moth Galls
Goldenrod galls are one of the most common galls found in winter. (A) The elliptical goldenrod gall is formed by the larva of a moth (*Gnorimoschema gallaesolidagunis*). (B) Close-up view. (C) Goldenrod ball gall formed by the larva of a small spotted-winged fly *Eurosta solidaginis*.

stem, lengthwise, through the gall. Carefully pry apart the stem and observe the silk cocoon constructed by the moth larva. Use a pair of fine tweezers to remove a portion of this silk lining and place it on a clean, dry microscope slide. Place a drop of water on the silk and observe what happens. Research the proteins fibroin and sericin and their characteristics. Can you deduce the last part of the overwintering freeze-avoidance strategy?

Another insect, the gall fly (*Eurosta solidaginis*), also inhabits the goldenrod plant, but it produces rounded ball-like galls. Its overwintering strategy is freeze tolerance—producing a cocktail of cryoprotectants as well as ice nucleators that allow it to survive the frozen embrace.

SOW BUGS

If you have ever lifted a rock or piece of rotting wood, you have probably come across the little animals called sow bugs or pill bugs. These bugs roll into a ball when touched.

Sow bugs are among the few land crustaceans—animals that have two pairs of antennae and breathe using gills. Typical aquatic crustaceans are lobsters, crayfish, crabs, and barnacles.

Scientists believe that sow bugs have special humidity receptors on their antennae. To learn more about this interesting feature, collect some sow bugs in damp places around gardens, fields, or wooded areas. Check under logs or stones, or leave a piece of burlap undisturbed on the ground for several days.

Keep the sow bugs in a pan that contains dirt covered with leaf litter and pieces of bark.

Now build a sowbug hygrometer. A hygrometer is a device that measures the humidity (water content) of air. Build or buy a shallow, rectangular, opaque plastic box 23 × 30 × 10 centimeters (9 × 12 × 4 in.). Plastic food storage containers will also work well.

Turn the cover into a piece of equipment that creates a different amount of humidity in different places. To do this, you will need the box's lid and some cotton.

Glue two long strips of cotton along the lid. Conduct a humidity test by wetting the cotton along half the lid's length. Place ten sow bugs in the middle of the box, close the cover, and record the number of sow bugs in the low-humidity zone (dry cotton) and in the high-humidity zone (wet cotton). Repeat this experiment four or five times. Which zone is preferred? To be sure the bugs aren't rearranging themselves in response to some other property of the box, run the experiment without wetting the cotton.

To see whether scientists are correct in asserting that the sow bug's antennae contain humidity receptors, use forceps to carefully remove the antennae from at least ten sow bugs. What happens when you perform the experiment again? If the bugs seem sensitive to humidity, cover other parts of the sow bugs with petroleum jelly to shield them from the air. What happens now?

When you run the second group of experiments, be sure to include control bugs—bugs that haven't been operated on or greased.

Do you better understand why sow bugs prefer damp places?

- Investigate other insects to see if they are sensitive to humidity. Can you find animals that prefer dryness? Why would any animal prefer a lack of humidity?

CHAPTER 7

VERTEBRATES— ANIMALS WITH BACKBONES

Think "animal," and one of a multitude of familiar images may appear: dog, cat, bird, frog, fish—even yourself. Indeed, these are all animals, and although very different from one another, they all have something in common: Each has an internal bony support structure called a *skeleton*. Animals without such a support structure are called invertebrates, animals without backbones. These organisms include insects, slugs, and worms. Some invertebrates, such as shellfish, have external skeletons, or *exoskeletons*.

Vertebrates are but a small portion of the animal kingdom. What they lack in representative numbers, though, they more than compensate for in complexity. All but a few microscopic forms have a brain and a nerve cord. Their complexity and other attributes make them very adaptable, and vertebrates occupy every type of habitat on

Earth. In short, vertebrates make excellent subjects of study.

Be sure to study *Guiding Principles for Use of Animals in Elementary and Secondary Schools*, available from the Humane Society of the United States. By following these guidelines, you will be sure of properly treating vertebrates and other life-forms and also of qualifying your project for a science fair. Science fairs usually have strict rules governing projects involving vertebrates. You can obtain the guidelines by writing to the society at 2100 L Street NW, Washington, DC 20037, or by visiting the website at http://www.hsus.org.

BONES

You can learn about vertebrates by studying their skeletons. If you can, visit a local museum or nature center to observe skeleton preparations. Local state conservation offices are usually helpful. Taxidermists are another excellent source of prepared bones that are safe to handle. Never handle bones found outside in the field without wearing gloves unless a knowledgeable adult says it's safe.

- Investigate the structure, shapes, and strength of bones from different animals. Which ones are solid? Which are hollow? Which are the strongest? Can you find a reason that explains the structure or shape of each bone? Does an overriding principle seem to be at work?
- Collect and compare examples of external skeletons of invertebrates (such as clam shells) with skeletons of common eating fare (such as chickens and cows). Which are strongest? Lightest? Can you make a generalization about structural differences between

vertebrates and invertebrates with exoskeletons? Do you think the form (shape) of the bones or shells is a result of their function? In other words, do certain bones have a certain shape so that they can serve a particular purpose?

YOUR FEET ARE TOO BIG— OR ARE THEY?

Animals leave tracks. Knowing how to identify these tracks can tell you a great deal about the animal that made them.

Why can a bird walk on top of a snowdrift or mud flat, when you would sink into it? Because the ratio of the bird's weight to the size of its feet is less than the ratio of your weight to your foot size. This ratio is called the *sink factor*. Sink factor is calculated using the following formula:

$$\frac{\text{Weight (in grams)}}{\text{Foot area (in square centimeters)}}$$

To calculate the sink factor of a snowshoe hare, for example, you would measure its prints and redraw them on graph paper, as shown in Figure 33. Then you would find the number of square centimeters occupied by the prints. In this case, the front feet are 20 square centimeters and the hind feet are 76 square centimeters, for a total of 96 square centimeters. Since a snowshoe hare weighs 1.5 kilograms (3 pounds), the sink factor is

$$\frac{1.5 \text{ kg}}{96 \text{ cm}^2}$$

or 0.016

You can see that a much heavier animal with feet of the same size would have a much larger sink factor. For example, an animal weighing 96 kilograms (211 lb.) that had the same print sizes would have a sink factor of 1. Conversely, an animal that weighs less and has the same print size will have a much smaller sink factor. What size sink factor would an animal with bigger feet and the same weight have? Less weight?

When measuring the combined area of an animal's footprints, you can either make a cast of the prints and measure the cast or simply measure the prints directly.

Make casts of animal tracks by pouring plaster of paris into a suitable mold (a can or container that is open on both ends) large enough to cover the footprint to a depth of 2 to 3 centimeters (1 in.). Wait 4 to 6 hours for the cast to dry. Apply ink to the cast and use it as a stamp to make an impression on graph paper as an aid in taking sink-

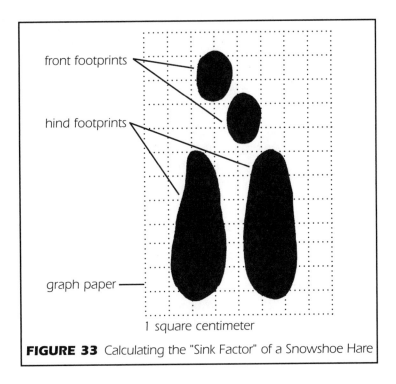

front footprints

hind footprints

graph paper

1 square centimeter

FIGURE 33 Calculating the "Sink Factor" of a Snowshoe Hare

factor measurements. In snow, sprinkle the tracks with water, which will harden as ice, forming a "mold." Then mix surrounding snow with plaster of paris and pour the mixture into the track mold to make the plaster casting. You may also wish to use melted paraffin wax poured in thin layers to make casts of mud tracks.

You can do some of the following projects using books or working in the field.

- Calculate your own sink factor with and without skis, snowshoes, or diving fins. Do these adaptations make a difference?
- Study different birds, especially shore and aquatic birds. What adaptations (if any) help birds reduce their sink factor?
- Use guides to predict which animals are best adapted to walking on snow. If possible, do fieldwork to test your prediction. Are snowshoe hares really better adapted to walking on snow than other rabbits?
- When you find tracks, try to identify the animal that made them and figure out if the animal was running or walking, whether it has claws or hooves, and whether it was digging or pawing. Are there lots of animals of one type in the area? Can you find any killing sites, with feathers, blood, and signs of a fight?

BIRD MIGRATION

Every winter, when temperatures drop in northern latitudes, billions of birds migrate south to warmer climates. And every spring, when temperatures rise up north, these same birds fly north to their breeding grounds, sometimes returning to within half a kilometer of where they were born.

Bird migration, though predictable, is poorly understood and continues to puzzle scientists. Depending on where you live, you should be able to observe bird migrations. Keep track of migration in early spring and again in early autumn. The best time of the day to do your observing is in the early morning.

In early spring, make a list of the permanent residents—those birds that do not migrate. This will allow you to keep track of the migrants.

Visit different habitats, such as forests, the shore, swamps, lakes, and fields. As you observe, take careful notes. Remember that each bird has its own schedule and characteristic migration pattern. Your observations could take note of the following:

- Do birds arrive at day or at night? Does the size of the bird have anything to do with its arrival time?
- When does each species arrive and depart?
- Do arriving or departing birds fly singly or in groups?
- Are both sexes around at the same time in spring?
- Can you find a flyway—a path that all incoming and outgoing birds seem to take—near you? Use reference books and the Web to locate flyways.
- Do any birds come to your area for the winter?

Join Project Feederwatch. Counting birds is key to helping scientists monitor their status. Call 1-800-843-BIRD.

YOUR BEAK IS WHAT YOU EAT

Is beak shape related to diet?

Observe birds eating seeds, worms, fish, rodents, and so on. Examine trees for signs of bird activity (for example, woodpeckers leave holes). Take careful notes detailing what you observe. How many beak shapes can you find and draw? What do you conclude?

ANIMAL BEHAVIOR

Study a wild animal in its natural habitat. Include in your observations its response to its own species, to other species, and to the nonliving environment. Pay attention to feeding, courtship, and defense of itself, its young, and its territory. Also note the way it communicates with other members of its species and with other species, as well as how it responds to external stimuli (wind, moisture, temperature, and light).

Try to observe the animal without being seen. If possible, use binoculars or a field scope. If you can, take pictures or use a video camera to record behavior. Take detailed notes in a field notebook.

PROBING OWL PELLETS

Owls and other birds of prey routinely regurgitate the undigested remains (bones, skin, and feathers) of their prey. The study of these pellets is an interesting way to investigate the bird's diet and the distribution of the small mammals they eat.

You can buy owl pellets from biological supply companies (see the Appendix), collect your own, or obtain them from zoos or aviaries. The most common owl pellets come from barn owls (*Tyto alba*), medium-size owls whose range extends virtually around the world, with the exception of deserts and arctic tundra. They nest in a variety of locales, ranging from church steeples and caves to silos and hollow trees. Barn owls typically feed on various rodents; larger mammals, such as rabbits; insects, including grasshoppers and beetles; and small birds, such as blackbirds.

WHO EATS WHOM

All organisms are biochemical machines that are powered by energy captured from the sun through photosynthesis. Naturalists assign every organism in an ecosystem to a *trophic level* based on what it eats. The organisms that first capture the sun's energy are called *producers*. They make energy-storing molecules. Producers include plants, some types of protists, and bacteria. All other organisms in an ecosystem are *consumers*. They obtain energy by consuming producers. A special class of consumers that obtain their energy from the organic wastes and dead bodies of all other organisms are *decomposers*. A graphic representation of this "who eats whom" relationship is called a *food chain* and is described in detail in the table on the next page.

The sum of these interconnecting networks of food chains is a *food web*—a graphic picture of how energy and materials move through a community.

Dissecting an Owl Pellet

1. Create a labeled prey plate that has pie-shaped areas as illustrated in Figure 34.
2. Place the owl pellet in the center of a newspaper.
3. Use the pointed end of a pencil to help you break apart the owl pellet. Be especially careful to not damage small bones as you work.
4. As each bone is uncovered, carefully use a toothpick to help you remove hair and other debris. Place the bone on the prey plate in its correct group. Use the Guide to Common Owl Prey, Figure 35, as an aid in identifying bone types. Be alert! You may have more than a single prey organism in your pellet.

WHO EATS WHOM

Trophic levels

Producers: Green plants manufacture food from light energy.

Consumers:

Herbivores are plant feeders.

Carnivores consume herbivores.

Omnivores consume both plant and animal matter and act as scavengers.

Decomposers are microorganisms (bacteria and fungi) that break down remains and wastes of organisms.

owl	eats	Field Mice, Voles, Birds, Shrews, Moles, Lizards, Grasshoppers, Moths, Beetles
bird	eats	Seeds, Grasshoppers, Moths, Beetles
field mouse	eats	Grass, Seeds, Grasshoppers, Moths, Beetles
vole	eats	Plant Roots, Grass, Seeds, Grasshoppers, Moths, Beetles
shrew	eats	Grasshoppers, Moths, Beetles
mole	eats	Grasshoppers, Moths, Beetles
lizard	eats	Seeds, Flowers, Grasshoppers, Moths, Beetles
grasshopper	eats	Plants, Seeds
beetle	eats	Plants, Flowers, Seeds
moth	eats	Flowers
mushroom	eats	Organic Materials, Dead Bodies
soil bacteria	eats	Organic Materials, Dead Bodies

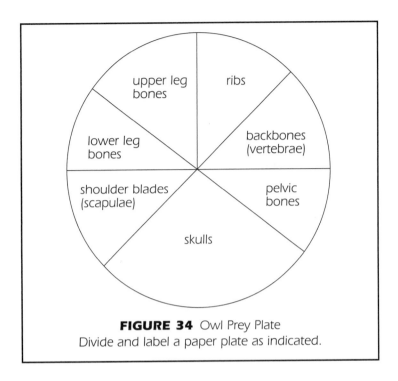

FIGURE 34 Owl Prey Plate
Divide and label a paper plate as indicated.

Undigested insects, such as beetles, pill bugs, and other forms, may have invaded the pellet before it was collected. Do not count them as prey. Soak bones in household bleach to remove stains.

Caution: Careful! Avoid getting these chemicals on your skin or in your eyes.

5. Use the two-answer (dichotomous) key to identify prey animals removed from the pellet.

Other Pellet Projects

- Select bones from the prey plate to reconstruct a half-skeleton of a rodent or bird prey animal on a clean paper plate. Use white glue to affix the bones to the paper plate. Leave spaces for missing bones. Use

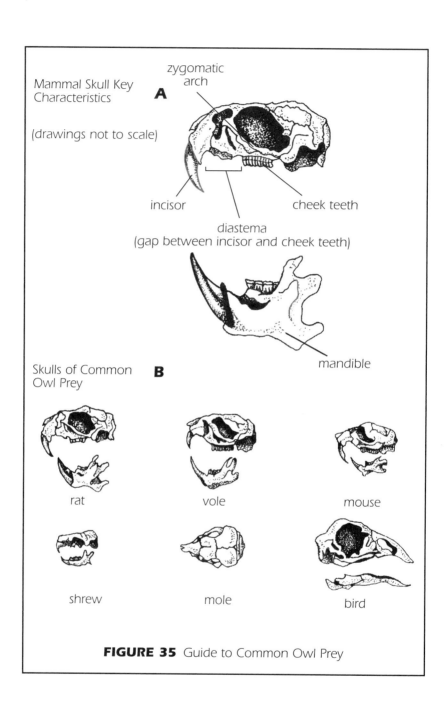

Mammal Skull Key Characteristics **A**

(drawings not to scale)

zygomatic arch

incisor

cheek teeth

diastema
(gap between incisor and cheek teeth)

mandible

Skulls of Common Owl Prey **B**

rat

vole

mouse

shrew

mole

bird

FIGURE 35 Guide to Common Owl Prey

1a Prey is bony material (skull) → Go to 2
1b Prey is not bony material → Insect

2a Skull has teeth → Mammal → Go to 3
2b Skull has no teeth → Bird

3a Skull has a gap between the incisor and cheek teeth
(diastema) → (order Rodentia) → Go to 5
3b Skull has no gap between the incisor and cheek
teeth (diastema) → (order Insectivora) → Go to 4

4a Skull has zygomatic arch, is flat and broad in shape
→ mole (*Scapanus*)
4b Skull has no zygomatic arch, is not flat or broad in
shape → shrew (*Sorex*)

5a Skull is generally flat and broad, cheek teeth are
angled, may appear as one continuous tooth → vole
(*Microtus*)
5b Skull is generally rounded, cheek teeth rounded and
distinct → Go to 6

6a Length of lower jaw is 10 to 15 mm → mouse →
Go to 7
6b Length of lower jaw is 17 to 30 mm → rat (*Rattus*)

7a Upper incisor is distinctly grooved → harvest mouse
(*Reithrodontomys*)
7b Upper incisor is smooth, not grooved → Go to 8

8a Cheek teeth are capped with enamel → house
mouse (*Mus*)
8b Cheek teeth are not capped with enamel → deer
mouse (*Peromyscus*)

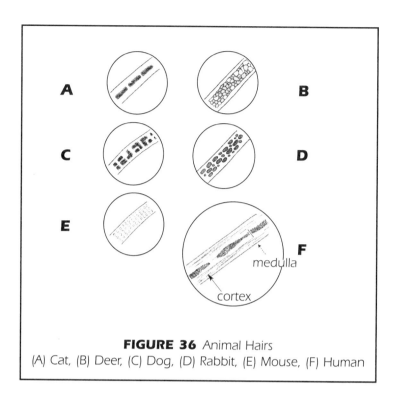

FIGURE 36 Animal Hairs
(A) Cat, (B) Deer, (C) Dog, (D) Rabbit, (E) Mouse, (F) Human

rodent or bird skeleton diagrams in reference books as a guide during your reconstruction.

- Make a dry mount of animal hairs recovered from your owl pellet. View these hairs at 100X magnification. Draw what you see in your notebook. Pay particular attention to each hair's center, or *medullary core*. Use Figure 36 as a guide. Generally, animal hair has a medullary index greater than 0.5—i.e., the diameter of the medulla is 50 percent plus the diameter of the hair. Human hair, by comparison, has a medullary index of 0.33.

FISH BEHAVIOR

Many interesting projects can be done with fish. You can obtain many fish from aquarium shops. Fish can also be observed in streams, lakes, and the ocean.

SCHOOLING

A school of fish is a leaderless and close-knit group moving at the same pace and engaging in the same activity.

- Fill two 1-liter (1-qt.) mayonnaise jars half full of water from a 10-gallon aquarium. Add 12 neon tetras (a type of tropical fish) to one jar and one tetra to the other jar. Fill to the top with aquarium water and seal with the lids. Place the jars, inverted, in the aquarium at opposite ends. Introduce a single neon tetra into the middle of the aquarium. What happens? Repeat this part of the experiment by changing the number of fish in the jars. Do neons school? Experiment with other fish. Be sure to release the fish from the jars after experimenting.
- If you are near a river, lake, or tide pool, can you observe any schools of fish? Sometimes huge schools of fish (such as anchovies, bluefish, and salmon) can be seen in rivers and oceans. Investigate massive runs of fish like these.
- Can you affect schooling behavior with different types of lighting, magnetic fields, sound waves, music, different-colored water, or other stimuli?

AGGRESSION

African cichlids and bettas, familiar in aquarium shops, are fish that display aggressive behavior. Devise experiments that show aggressive behavior (such as raised gill covers, tail beating, and fin spreading) among the same and opposite sexes of these species when they are placed in individual, transparent containers set next to each other.

Investigate the effects on aggressive behavior of temperature, colors, drawings or models, light, outside movement, and so on. Do these fish react to seeing themselves in a mirror? If they do, how much of their image must they see to react?

LEARNING

Do fish use color to locate their food? You can find out by trying the following experiment.

Keep a single goldfish alone in an aquarium. Obtain or make three disks (using any waterproof material, such as tiddledywinks), each about 1.5 centimeters (0.5 in.) in diameter, of three different colors. Glue each disk to a stick or wire.

Drape tubifex red worms (food for the goldfish) around one of the colored disks and immerse all three disks simultaneously in the water to the same depth.

Repeat this procedure three times a day for two or three days, always placing the food around the same disk. On the fourth day, introduce the colored disks without food.

- What happens? Why? Experiment with different disk colors. If the fish seem to respond to color, how do you know they aren't just responding to the location of the food?
- Can you train fish to locate food in other ways, through lures or scents?

LIGHT AND REPRODUCTION

Find out whether high-intensity white light affects reproduction in guppies. Does it affect courtship, fertility, egg development, egg-laying ability, and so on?

TEMPERATURE AND BEHAVIOR

Use goldfish or guppies to study the effects of temperature on fish. The best way to change the temperature in an aquarium is to immerse plastic bags of hot water or ice cubes into the aquarium water. Never let the temperature exceed 30° C (85° F) or go below 14° C (55° F).

- Does temperature affect behavior such as rate of gill beating, courtship and reproduction (in guppies), or overall health?
- In guppies, does temperature favor the development of one sex over the other? Sex can be distinguished by comparing the distance between the anal and pelvic fins. This distance is longer in females than it is in males.

ENVIRONMENT AND GROWTH

Does environment affect the rate of growth? Test the effects of crowding, quantity and quality of food, and stimuli such as light, temperature, pH, sound, water movement, and magnetism on growth. Use fast-growing tropical fish like guppies for your investigations. For example, you may want to observe the effect of different light colors (particularly red, blue, and green) by covering the outside of the tank with colored plastic sheets.

MUTUAL DEFENSE

There is safety in numbers. Animals often form groups to protect themselves from predators.

Investigate the phenomenon of flock defense. Construct a model of a predator (like a hawk) and rig it so that it will "fly" down a wire toward a bait site (scattered birdseed) that attracts many birds of the same species. If you can, use a video camera to record bird reactions—

especially if the device has slow-motion capability. What flock size has the quickest reaction time to the model threat? Do the birds ever attack the model?

DECOYS

Find out whether decoys like scarecrows and rooftop "owls" really work.

A TURTLE'S EAR AND OTHER TALES

Can turtles hear? And if so, how?

First, try to answer the first question. In your experiment, make sure you test all kinds of sounds, from whispering to bells, low sounds to very high sounds, loud and soft, and so on.

Find out whether the turtle uses its shell to help it hear. Since the body of a turtle is mostly a bony shell, devise ways that sound vibrations can pass through the shell to monitor an effect. You might want to place a turtle on a thin piece of plywood. Place the plywood over an upturned speaker. You will then be able to transmit various sound frequencies (as vibrations) through the plywood to the turtle's shell. Always be mindful of never creating too loud a sound or frequency vibration that will overly excite or harm the animal.

When you're through experimenting with turtles, you may want to experiment with yourself or your friends, being careful not to risk damaging anyone's hearing by exposing them to sounds that are too loud or too high in frequency. Try the following activities while wearing earplugs.

- Place a stick between your teeth and vibrate it. Can you hear it? Now vibrate it at arm's length. Can you hear anything now?

- Try the same using a rubber band. Hold the rubber band against the bone next to your ear on your cheek. Now vibrate the rubber band at arm's length. What happens? Is this similar to the turtle's way of hearing?

A CLOSER LOOK AT AMPHIBIANS

Amphibians generally live on land, but return to the water to reproduce. Some familiar amphibians are frogs, toads, and salamanders. Amphibians are interesting vertebrates to study because of their ability to adapt to many environments.

NATURAL POPULATION CONTROL

Some animals seem to regulate the number of their young that mature. Find out whether this is the case with frogs.

Place one or two large tadpoles in a jar or aquarium with a group of much smaller tadpoles. Include a number of *Elodea* plants (available in pet shops) or pieces of lettuce as food. Over the next week, observe and record tadpole behavior.

Prepare another jar with small tadpoles, and into this jar pour the water from a jar containing much larger tadpoles. What happens? What do you think causes what you observed? Is it a chemical substance secreted by tadpoles themselves? Does diluting the water have any effect?

Consider the meaning of this effect in nature at times when food is scarce. Can you achieve the same effect in any other way or with other animals such as fish?

CAMOUFLAGE

- *Melanocytes* are pigment cells in the skin of amphibians and other vertebrates. By contracting or expanding, these cells can alter skin shade to help camouflage the animal. Observe different amphibians (such as the leopard frog, *Rana pipiens;* salamanders; toads; and newts) against backgrounds of different colors in zoos, pet shops, or in the wild. Do a survey of which amphibians use camouflage, which are most successful, and whether they form different colors.

- Place frog tadpoles in tanks covered by colored plastic sheets. Compare a light color with a dark color. Be sure to include *Elodea*, or a similar aquatic plant for food. Do the animals develop a different skin color in each rearing condition?

GROWTH AND DEVELOPMENT

Study the effects of temperature, water quality (pond water versus storm-water runoff from a parking lot), light (colored plastic sheets), and other environmental factors on amphibian development. Collect egg masses (bunches of slimy strings or jelly masses) floating or attached to pieces of grass or twigs at the edges of ponds or other shallow waters. Place the egg masses in an aquarium to incubate and hatch tadpoles. Use a hand lens to observe individual eggs removed from the aquarium and placed in a shallow dish. Investigate the effect of low temperatures on egg development by using your refrigerator and comparing development with similar eggs kept at room temperature in an aquarium.

FIELD STUDIES

In the spring, try to identify which amphibian breeds first by watching for egg masses. Use field guides to help identify amphibian egg masses.

- Listen for amphibian mating calls. How far do they carry? Does one male's call affect other males? What time of day are frog calls most often heard? Do weather conditions affect breeding behavior?

CHAPTER 8

NATURE
AT LARGE

Al organisms on Earth occupy small niches where
they interact with other organisms and with the
environment. All organisms are also part of a greater system—the *biosphere*, the fragile shell within which all life
exists. For example, the fly buzzing inside your window is
not only part of the local habitat, which includes you,
your dog, the garbage out back, and the lawn in front. It
is also part of the biosphere, which includes the oceans,
atmosphere, mountains, weather systems, and all life-
forms everywhere.

In recent years, the biosphere has come under
increasing attack from the effects and by-products of civ-
ilization. Threats have included degradation of the ozone
layer, acid rain, toxic waste and pesticides, soil erosion,
and radiation. Today, we are beginning to deal with these
challenges to the biosphere both in the scientific community and in the courts.

In this chapter, you will find projects that focus on the interrelationships between organisms and their environment.

SOIL—THE FORGOTTEN RESOURCE

Soil is a complex mixture of inorganic minerals (clay, silt, pebbles, and sand), decaying organic matter, water, air, and living organisms. It is the biosphere in miniature—host to a complex web of interconnected processes that renew and recycle. Like fossil fuels, it is nonrenewable, and its production takes a very long time. The Department of Agriculture estimates that about *6 billion tons* of soil from farmlands and development practices is lost to erosion each year! That's enough to cover the state of Rhode Island 30 centimeters (1 foot) deep! Here are some projects that will help you better understand just what a precious resource soil is.

WHAT'S ON THE HORIZON?

Every soil has a history that effects its vulnerability to erosion. Soil forms through weathering and other processes that act on *parent material*—bedrock or other geologic material. Nearly all soils develop a series of different *horizons* (layers). In most undisturbed soil, the major horizons are called the surface or *topsoil*, the *subsoil*, and the underlying parent material. Topsoil almost always has the highest organic content, subsoils have very low concentrations of organic material, and parent material has hardly any organic content.

- Locate and study soil horizons near where you live —an eroded road bank, a trench dug during construction, or a hole dug with a spade that has a smooth, straight face. Use a meter stick or a yardstick to measure each layer. Sketch the horizons in your field notebook. Be sure to include a scale so that horizon depths from various study locations can be compared.

SOIL PARTICLES ARE NOT CREATED EQUALLY

The size of soil particles is important. The amount of *interstitial space* (space between soil particles) determines just how fast water moves through soil or how much water soil will hold. The Wentworth Scale (see the table on the next page) details the relative progression of particle size and particle type. *Loam* refers to soils that have a favorable proportion of sand, silt, and clay—usually in equal amounts.

- Conduct a *soil stratification test* by filling a mason jar about two-thirds with water. Pour in dry soil until the jar is almost full. Replace the cover and shake the jar vigorously. Place the jar on a table and let the soil settle, allowing plenty of time (overnight) to allow the finest particles (clays) to settle. Hold a white index card against the side of the jar and draw a diagram of the various layers. Label each layer (clay, silt, sand) according to the descriptive terminology used in the Wentwort Scale. Use a ruler to record the various depths of each layer in each sample. Calculate the percentage by diving each particle type by the overall sediment depth. For example, a 2.5-centimeter (1-in.) sample has a sand layer measuring 5 millimeters (0.19 in.). The percent sand composition of the sample would be 20 percent.
- Sample other soils in the same manner. Compare and contrast your results in your field notebook. Try to obtain samples that illustrate as many Wentworth

WENTWORTH SCALE

Particle Size (mm)	Particle Type
>4	Pebble, cobble, boulder
2–4	Granule
1–2	Very coarse sand
0.5–1	Coarse sand
0.25–0.5	Medium sand
0.125–0.25	Fine sand
0.0625–0.125	Very fine sand
0.004–0.0625	Silt
<0.004	Clay

Scale types as possible as well as various combinations of clay, silt, and sand.

HOW FAST DOES IT PERC?

Percolation is the movement of water through soil. Percolation tests (also known as perc tests) are usually made to determine whether soils are suitable for septic systems. Good *infiltration* (downward movement of water from the surface of the land to subsoils) is the hallmark of a good perc test. Soils are placed in four hydrologic (water infiltration) groups and are given letter designations according to a soil classification system.

GROUP A   Sands/gravels—soils with high infiltration rates.

GROUP B Fine to moderate textures (sandy loam)— soils with moderate infiltration rates.

GROUP C Clay loams—sandy soils high in clay—soils moderately fine in texture—soils with slow infiltration rates.

GROUP D Clays—soils with very slow infiltration rates.

• Conduct perc (soil permeability) tests at various locales near where you live. Be sure to get permission before digging any holes. Use a trowel or spade to dig a hole approximately 30 centimeters (12 in.) deep and 15 centimeters (6 in.) in diameter. Insert a wooden or plastic ruler into the hole. Pour water into the hole to a depth of 17.5 centimeters (7 in.). (A plastic milk jug is a handy carrier; you will need at least two of them.) Allow the water to drop an initial inch to saturate the soil. In your field notebook, record the time (in minutes) that it takes for the remaining 15 centimeters (6 in.) of water poured to infiltrate the soil. Set up a table that compares perc rate (inches per unit time) to hydrologic soil group. For example, a 15-centimeter (6-in.) column of water infiltrated into sandy (group A) soil in 12 minutes has a perc rate of 15 centimeters (6 in.) ÷ 12 minutes, or 1.25 centimeters (0.5 in.) per minute. Generally, soil scientists consider soil to have an acceptable perc rate if infiltration of a 15-centimeter (6-in.) column of water occurs within 1 hour.

GROUND COVER—THE FIRST LINE OF DEFENSE AGAINST EROSION

Living plants, plant residue (mulch), and bits of rock on the surface of the soil intercept falling raindrops and absorb some erosive energy before the drops reach the soil. Vegetative ground cover also slows the flow of water across the surface and increases the rate at which water infiltrates (soaks into) the soil.

- Study the erosion energy of raindrops by constructing splash boards. Obtain two pine boards 2.5 centimeters (1 in.) thick, 10 centimeters (4 in.) wide, and 105 centimeters (3.5 ft) long. Sharpen one end of each board. Paint them white. Mark lines across the boards at 30-centimeter (1-ft) intervals beginning at the unsharpened end. Attach 10-centimeter (4-in.) (square) pieces of galvanized metal to the top of each board to prevent rain from washing off splashed soil.
- Locate a splash board on bare ground (along a path in a schoolyard) and on a grassy spot without any exposed soil. Drive the splash boards into these selected locations to a depth of 15 centimeters (6 in.). Leave them there and observe them after the first rain. You can also simulate rain by sprinkling the ground with water from a sprinkling can. Hold the can at a height of 1 to 1.5 meters (3 to 5 ft) above the ground. Record the height of soil splashes.

EROSION CONTROL STRATEGIES

For more than 50 years, farmers have been practicing soil conservation methods designed to minimize soil loss. Do the following projects to learn more about how crop cover, mulching, and contour plowing reduce soil erosion. Use Figure 37 as your guide.

What You Need
Utility knife
5 shoe boxes lined with plastic sheeting

Topsoil or garden soil

Sod pieces

Garden mulch

Pencil

Wood blocks or similar supports

5 buckets

Watering can or a coffee can punched with small holes

What You Do

1. Use a utility knife to cut a V-shaped notch in each shoe box to function as a spout.
2. Fill box 1 with firmly packed moist soil, box 2 with sod, box 3 with moist soil packed firmly and covered with garden mulch, box 4 with moist soil packed firmly with furrows (made with a pencil) running lengthwise, and box 5 with three strips of packed moist soil alternating with three strips of sod running crosswise.
3. Position the boxes on supports so that they are all on the same incline. Place buckets under the spouts to collect the water and sediment runoff.
4. Sprinkle water steadily for 5 seconds onto each box. In your field notebook, record the amount of time the water continues to flow from the spout of each box. After the water has run off, measure the amount of sediment collected from each bucket.

Which land practice(s) seem best for reducing soil erosion? Research other soil conservation practices to evaluate.

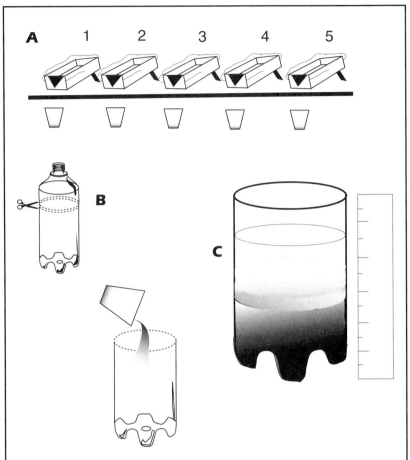

FIGURE 37 Erosion Control Strategies

(A) Create five land profiles, all having the same slope angle (e.g. 15°). Use a watering can to apply equal volumes (e.g. 1/2 gallon) of simulated "rainwater." from a height of 12 inches, to each land profile. Use a bucket or similar container top capture any runoff that occurs. (B) Cut the top from a 2-liter soda bottle to create a sediment gauge. For each land profile, thoroughly mix and pour all the collected runoff into the sediment gauge. (C) Use a ruler to record both the height of the water column and the sediment layer. Poor erosion control measures will yield the highest amount of sediment and runoff volume.

OTHER PROJECTS

- Simulate construction on steep slopes by constructing mounds of soil in the middle of plastic-lined boxes or in two large round pie tins or dishpans. With a pencil or finger, make furrows up and down one side of the mound and in circles around the other. Calculate the respective slopes for each mound. Sprinkle an equal amount of water over each mound and observe the water and soil runoff patterns created. Sketch these patterns in your notebook.
- If possible, visit some local areas that suffer from erosion, either natural or through poor land-management practices. Prepare a plan to repair the damage and prevent future loss of soil. You may want to use a camera or camcorder for this work.

STUDYING A STREAM'S LOAD

The amount of material a stream carries at one time is its *load*. Streams transport this materials in one of three ways: in solution, in suspension, and bed load. In the United States alone, it is estimated that nearly 300 tons of dissolved material (minerals) are carried to the seas by streams each year. Multiply that by 4 billion years and you get an idea of why the oceans are salty.

THE INVISIBLE LOAD

The water picks up this invisible load as it courses over and through the land. Water is said to be hard or soft based on the amount of dissolved salts (such as magnesium and/or calcium carbonate) it contains.

- Hard- or soft-water streams are classified based on the mineral content of the water. Because these minerals (calcium and magnesium) are so abundant, hard-water streams usually exhibit *primary production* (microlife growth and oxygen production). Soft-water streams are just the opposite—they are nutrient-poor and have little primary production.

- Use a soil test kit (available at local garden centers) to test for the presence of carbonates. Make trips into the field and sample various streams to determine whether they are hard or soft—whether they are rich in carbonates or not.
- Water hardness is the water's capacity to precipitate soap out of solution. The degree of hardness can be assessed by the amount of lather remaining after shaking a soapy solution for five minutes. Conduct this test using two antacid tablets (with either magnesium or calcium carbonate as the active ingredient) allowed to dissolve in a mason jar two-thirds full of water. (Crushing helps tablets to dissolve better.) Fill another mason jar with a similar amount of water. Add a small (but equal) amount of soap (not detergent) to each jar. Agitate both jars for approximately five minutes. Compare the relative amount of suds in both jars of water. Give other collected water samples the hardness shake test—comparing relative hardness against the antacid standard.

SUSPENDED SOLIDS

A stream's load is deposited when its velocity falls below the point necessary to hold suspended particles (i.e., when a stream empties into a larger body of water) and the load settles to the bottom as sediment depending upon particle size. That is why civil engineers design deep areas (furboys) in ponds to catch stream loads.

- To investigate sediment deposition, you will need a number of tall, narrow jars (such as olive jars) with caps. After a heavy rain, fill one of the jars from a small stream that gets at least part of its water from cultivated fields and/or is directly downstream from a construction project. Find another stream where all the water drains from woodlands and another from an established pasture or meadow. Use topographic maps, if necessary, to help make determinations concerning drainage sources. Try and capture water from as close to the stream's middle as possible.

  Allow each of the water samples to settle for a few days. Observe them daily and record what you see in your field notebook. Find out how much a sample weighs by filtering and drying the sample. Use Figure 38 as a guide.

  Which drainage conditions result in the least sedimentation? The most? If possible, trace the water course to find the point of erosion. Use a camera and draw detailed maps to document field conditions.

BED LOAD

Particles too large (see the Wentworth Scale in this chapter) to be carried in suspension are bounced along the stream bottom with the ebb and flow (the rising and falling) of the stream's velocity. Such material is the stream's *bed load*.

- Sample stream beds to locate where bed loading occurs.

OTHER PROJECTS
- Take additional samples using a jar or similar container to "grab" a water sample from the approximate

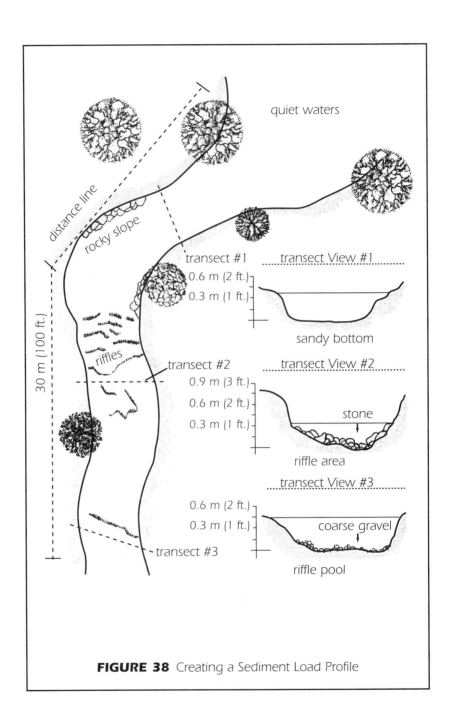

quiet waters

distance line

rocky slope

30 m (100 ft.)

riffles

transect #1

0.6 m (2 ft.)
0.3 m (1 ft.)

transect View #1

sandy bottom

transect #2

0.9 m (3 ft.)
0.6 m (2 ft.)
0.3 m (1 ft.)

transect View #2

stone

riffle area

transect View #3

0.6 m (2 ft.)
0.3 m (1 ft.)

coarse gravel

transect #3

riffle pool

FIGURE 38 Creating a Sediment Load Profile

middle (width and depth) of the stream—every hour if possible—to construct a *sedimentation load profile* for a given stream drainage during a 12- to 48-hour period following a heavy rain. Use Figure 38 as a guide in determining a stream's sediment load. To calculate a stream's sediment load:

1. Mark off 30 meters (100 ft.) with stakes along the length of a stream.
2. Find the average depth of a stream within this 30-meter (100-ft.) section. Wade into the stream and measure its depth along three points, or *transects*. Divide the total of the three depth measurements by 3 to get the average stream depth.
3. Find out how fast the water is moving. Throw a stick 5 or 8 centimeters (2 or 3 in.) long into the water above the upstream 30-meter (100-ft.) marker. Record the number of seconds it takes to float between the markers. Perform the following calculation:

    30 meters ÷ time (seconds) = speed of stick (in meters per second)

4. Find the average width of the measured stream section. Use a tape measure to measure the width of the stream at each of the three transects. Divide by 3 to get the average width of the stream.
5. To find flow volume, multiply the average width × the average depth × the number of meters the stick floated each second. This will tell you the number of cubic meters of water flowing in the stream every second.
6. Multiply the flow volume by the weight (in grams) of the sample per volume collected to arrive at the amount of sediment carried by the stream every second.

- If possible, trace the course of streams that empty into larger bodies of water. Can you observe silt deposition?

A STUDY IN SUCCESSION

A *biome* is an area that has a distinctive plant cover. The eruption of Mount St. Helens in 1980 destroyed part of the coniferous biome, leaving the region looking like a moonscape. Given enough time (perhaps a thousand years), the region will return to a climax (stable) community of conifers.

You can observe succession on a shorter time scale. Succession, or the replacement of one community by another, takes place in gradual stages, each with its own particular vegetation type, all the way to climax vegetation characterizing the biome. Begin by observing bare earth (recently cleared land), or clear a small lot (after obtaining permission) in a particular community of the biome in which you live. Observe which life-forms (weeds, lichens, insects) first appear. Take notes, make drawings, and take photographs of the area throughout the observation period. To speed things up, try to find other areas that were once cleared (a couple of years previously) and observe which plants are now in evidence. Has the animal life changed as well? In comparing these different locations at various stages of succession, do you observe differences in certain plant and animal populations between study areas? Make a chart that lists the changes and illustrate it with photographs.

INVESTIGATING STORM WATER RUNOFF

The Environmental Protection Agency (EPA) has calculated that runoff from the first hour of a moderate to heavy storm in a typical U.S. city will contribute more pollution load than would the city's untreated sanitary sewage during the same time period. Contaminants contained in urban and suburban runoff such as sediments, salt, phosphorous, nitrates, coliform bacteria, and lead and other heavy metals can impair water quality in streams, lakes, wetlands, and estuaries.

Investigate the environmental impacts of storm water runoff in areas where you live by doing one or all of these projects.

INVESTIGATING THE EFFECTS OF STORM WATER ON PLANTS

Use a kitchen baster to collect storm water samples from various locales (parking lots, city streets, paved urban/ rural roads etc.), and place them in quart-capacity mason jars and seal. Label each jar with the locality, duration and amount of rainfall, and time of collection. Study the effect of watering germinated bean seeds (or other plant types) with collected runoff water versus distilled water, used as a control. Use one 10-centimeter (4-in.) pot per collected sample type; plant 4 to 6 seeds per pot. Record your observations concerning percent germination, plant height and color in your field notebook.

- Calculate how much untreated storm water passes directly into streams, rivers, and other water bodies following a rain event without being allowed to infiltrate into soils or pass through wetland areas. (Approximately 0.6 gallon [2,270 mL] drains off a square foot of impervious surface following an inch of heavy rain.)

ROAD SALTING

In certain communities across the country, road salts are applied to road surfaces to melt snow and ice. Road salts are surface-active compounds, which raise the melting point of ice upon contact to facilitate travel on cold, wintry days.

- Study how road salts melt ice by placing equal amounts of commercially available de-icing products that use halite (sodium chloride), calcium chloride, or calcium magnesium acetate (CMA) on the top surfaces of equal-sized pieces of ice (such as ice cubes) at room temperature and observe the melting action. You may want to freeze identical samples of water in ice cube trays expose the frozen cubes (each placed in a bowl) to identical quantities of de-icing chemicals for a set period of time, and then measuring the amount of meltwater that was produced.
    - Record your observations in your notebook. Which de-icing material is the most efficient at melting ice at room temperature and at colder temperatures, such as those occurring inside a freezer compartment?
- Conduct "field trials" by applying various deicing materials to areas of a walkway or driveway and observing their action at various temperatures. Is calcium chloride a better low temperature de-icer than rock salt? Determine what temperature range is best for application of road salt to remove road ice.
- It is estimated that 182 kilograms (400 lbs.) of road salt is applied per dual-lane mile (twice that on hills) in geographic areas where its application is effective in melting ice and small layers of snow. This translates to, on average, 1.5 grams of salt per square foot of road surface (road lanes are usually 11 feet in width) applied on level dual-lane roads per salt run. The first inch of water (snow or rain) falling on a mile of imper-

vious dual-lane road surface will dissolve the salt and be carried away by sheet drainage. (About 2300 mL— 2/3 gallon of water per square foot runs off impervious surfaces following 1 inch of precipitation.)

- Contact the public works department to find out how many paved dual-lane miles exist in your town or county area. Calculate how much road salt is applied to county or town roads where you live.
- Water grass (and other plants) with a salt concentration equal to that washing off the road surface in a winter season (1.5 grams in 2300 mL times the number of seasonal applications). How does this concentration of salt affect plants? Can you observe similar vegetation appearances along roadsides in the spring?
- If possible, in the spring, locate a vegetated shoulder of roadway in your town that shows the effect of exposure to high salt concentrations. Look for a persistent brown appearance—even when there is green vegetation farther from the road. Measure the width of this "damage area" and compare it to other roadsides in other towns. Try to gather road salting data from each town's commissioner of public works. Do the observed physical effects (brown zone) compare to the discharge amounts of salt over a winter season?

  In urban areas, a large volume of this runoff is captured by storm sewers that direct captured flows to discharge points—usually rivers and streams with little, if any, pretreatment. Pollutants, like road salt, are thus directly discharged into water bodies like lakes and ponds. To get a feeling for the extent of this impact over time on a lake or pond, try this project.
- Add 10 milliliters (2 tsp.) of table salt (sodium chlo-

ride) to a glass of water. Stir until all the salt dissolves. Add a drop of blue food coloring to the salted water. Fill a mason jar half full with water. Slowly, allow the blue-colored salted water to flow from the glass down along the side of the mason jar. Observe what happens. Continue your observations over the next couple of days.

ACID RAIN

Acid rain is a term that denotes rain, snow, or other precipitation contaminated by acids. These rains form when water vapor in the air reacts with certain chemical compounds (nitrogen oxides and sulphur dioxides) from industrial, automotive, and power-generating sources. Environmental scientists use the term *acid deposition* to refer to both wet and dry acid pollution that falls to Earth.

What we call acid rain is any rain below a pH of 5.6. Most organisms live within a narrow pH range in their environments, so a pH change of one or two units can eliminate a great number of plants and animals. In acid lakes, where a variety of aquatic life once flourished, simpler plants and microalgae now exist. Dead leaves and twigs can become pickled rather than decomposing, preventing the release of nutrients back into the environment.

The change in pH also affects the chemical composition of the water. Many substances that are found in minute quantities reach abnormally high concentrations in acid lakes. Try some of these projects.

• Collect rainwater in cleaned containers at various times during a rainstorm (or snowstorm during winter months). Use pH paper (with a range of 5 to 9) to measure the pH. If possible, compare your data with data collected by friends in other cities that are sensitive to acid deposition.

- If possible, collect water samples from different lakes, ponds, or streams near you. Measure the pH and compare these values to commercial household products.

- Vinegar is used to preserve food like pickles and sauerkraut the acidity inhibits the decomposition of tissues. Some lakes are as acidic as vinegar. Place leaves (and other fruits or vegetables) in white vinegar and use a camera or video camera to record what happens over 4 to 6 weeks. Set up a control with the same items using just water.

- Each year, air pollutants cause millions of dollars of damage to plants, buildings, statuary, and stained glass. Marble is a form of calcium carbonate (calcite), a major building component. Obtain a small flake of white marble (ask the owner of a gravestone-monument or landscaping company for a small piece.) *Caution: Never alter or remove any material from gravestones or other building materials. Wear protective eyewear.* Place a small flake in a paper cup and add a small amount of white vinegar (5 to 7 percent acetic acid). Use a magnifying glass to examine the reaction. What effect does this acid solution have on marble? What is the gas being given off? If you live in or near a city on the East Coast, can you observe evidence of air-pollution degradation among buildings or statuary?

SURVIVAL OF AQUATIC ORGANISMS IN ACIDIC ENVIRONMENTS

(For Advanced Young Scientists)

Aquatic animals have varying sensitivities to inputs of acid in their habitats. This project explores how zooplankton react to acidification.

What You Need

Zooplankton net (see Figure 39 to make your own)

Collected pond (lake) water, bottom sediments, aquatic plants, and zooplankton

2 mason jars

pH paper (range 5–9)

Small measuring cup

White vinegar

Medicine dropper

What To Do

1. Use a zooplankton net (see Figure 39) to collect a variety of aquatic microlife forms from a nearby pond. Collect samples of pond or lake water as well as a jar of bottom sediments.

2. Create a miniature pond or lake ecosystem by placing a small layer of bottom sediments (no more than 1 centimeter [0.5 in.]) into a mason jar. Add collected water and aquatic plants. Place your pond/lake ecosystem near a window so that it will receive indirect (northern) sunlight.

3. Place approximately 25 each of various large zooplankton forms (use Figure 40 as a guide in

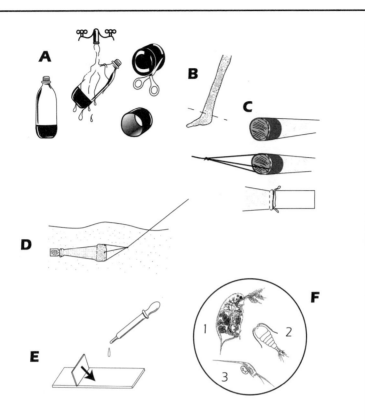

FIGURE 39 Making and Using a Zooplankton Net
(A) Use hot tap water to melt the glue adhesive holding the end-cap onto a plastic 2-liter soda bottle. (B) Use scissors to cut off the foot of a stocking. (C) Carefully staple the larger diameter end of the stocking to one end of the soda bottle end-cap. Use string to attach the smaller diameter end of the stocking to a plastic or glass vial. (D) Attach three guide lines to a central casting line. Cast your zooplankton net from a dock or a boat. Pull the net out of the water and allow all the water to drain out into the vial. Carefully remove the vial. (E) Use an eyedropper to collect a sample and make a wet mount. (F) Expect to observe large microcrustaceans such as (1) water flea (*Daphnia*), (2) copepods (*Cyclops*), and (3) rotifers (*Mesocyclops*).

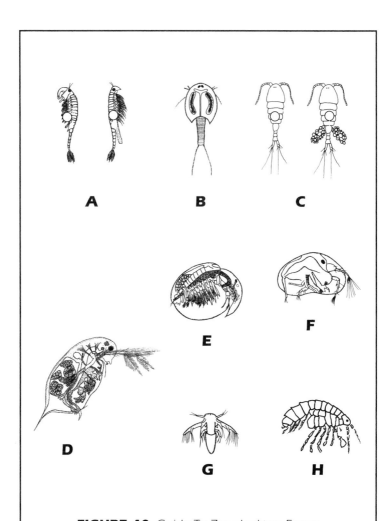

FIGURE 40 Guide To Zooplankton Forms
(A) Fairy shrimp 2.5-5cm (*Eubranchipus*, male / female), (B) Tadpole shrimp 2.5-5cm (Triops), (C) Copepod 1-2mm (*Cyclops* male / female), (D) Water flea 5mm (*Daphnia*), (E) Clam shrimp 2.5-5cm (*Lynceus*), (F) Seed shrimp 1.3mm (ostracod Cypricerus), (G) Microcrustacean nauplius stage larva 2mm (*Eubranchipus*), (H) Amphipod 12-15mm (*Hyalella*).

identification)—*Daphnia,* copepods, ostracods, amphipods—into your miniature pond/lake ecosystem. Record in your notebook which zooplankton forms were added as well as the pH of the collected water.

4. Prepare a control system—an identically sized mason jar containing an equal volume of collected water alone.

5. To each jar, slowly add 30 milliliters (1 oz.) of vinegar (equivalent of 5 to 7 percent acetic acid) using a medicine dropper. Use pH paper (or anthocyanin-extract paper) to measure the pH. Record pH values for both jars in your notebook. Add acid each day for one week or until the pH reaches 3.8 (the pH of most acid lakes). Record any mortality (death).

Analyzing Your Data

- Was the pH lowered (did acidity increase) in equal increments for both containers following the daily addition of vinegar? If not, design an additional experiment to identify the cause. Hint: In many cases, sediments contain dissolved substances that act as *buffers* ("chemical sponges" that have the ability to "soak up" added acids or bases so that the pH of a solution is little affected).

- Did certain organisms survive better than others? Which organisms are most sensitive to acidity?

MILKWEED

The perennial wildflower milkweed can be seen as patches of pinkish-purple colorings along roadsides, fields, and meadows throughout North America. The plant gets its name from the thick, milky white latex that it produces for defense against predators and that serves as a unique stage for observing ecological interrelationships.

Observe milkweed plants closely over several days and nights. Cover a flashlight with red cellophane to allow you to observe insects without disturbing them. Try to identify as many creatures as you can. Try to assign a food relationship (who eats whom) to the animals observed. Knowing what each organism does will help you construct a relationship diagram (a food web) for the milkweed plant community (the populations of organisms that live and interact in the same place). You should have no trouble identifying at least ten different species. Prepare a diagram or possibly a dried collection of various residents and visitors to the plant.

ESTABLISHING A NATURE TRAIL

One of the first self-guided nature trails was established in Bear Mountain State Park, Bear Mountain, New York, more than 50 years ago. There, the public was guided along a path to areas with posted signs instructing them on ecology and unique local geologic and ecologic conditions, along with exhibits that focused on the diversity and uniqueness of local area wildlife. For most of the viewers—residents of New York City—this was their first introduction to nature's landscape.

Creating a nature trail is rewarding and will serve to sharpen your powers of observation and increase your knowledge and awareness of our natural world. It is also hard work! Begin by obtaining the permission of the landowner; abide by whatever conditions the landowner sets forth regarding the use of the property. You must work under adult supervision. Enlist the aid of a science

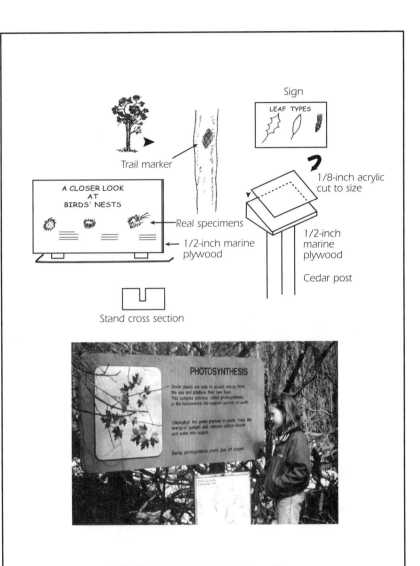

FIGURE 41 Trailside Nature Signs

Create your own trailside nature signs to highlight important environmental conditions along your nature trail. In the photograph, Caroline Rainis is getting trailside information at the Cummings Nature Center in Naples, New York.

teacher or other adult who is knowledgeable in the natural sciences.

- Begin by deciding what the objective of the trail will be. Will it inform viewers by identifying area vegetation, point out unique environmental features, be a study area for succession, or all of the above? Stake out the trail using stakes or colored buttons affixed to trees.
- Obtain field guides and other reference works (see the Appendix) to identify plants along the trail.
- Create signs that identify life-forms and unique natural geologic or ecologic conditions, or that simply point the way.
- Consider creating special dioramas, models, relief (topographic) maps, or displays that further explain and illustrate various natural aspects of your selected locality. For example, you may want to create a display of deciduous leaf types (as well as bark and winter twig samples) found along the trail or a collection of birds' nests or pinecones to enhance viewer understanding. These displays might be housed in a special area set up on "open trail" days during which you and your friends conduct special tours.
- Consider giving a special "video tour" by having a friend film you narrating a tour along the trail.

SOURCES OF MATERIAL

Most of the materials required for projects in this book are available at local stores. However, if you wish to expand your home laboratory or obtain a hard-to-find life form, the following firms offer science education materials. Specialized materials are also listed below. Most companies can be contacted on the Web; some have web-based catalogs that will make direct ordering easy!

Carolina Biological Supply Company
2700 York Road
Burlington, NC 27215
(800) 334-5551
http://www.carolina.com

Connecticut Valley Biological Supply Company
82 Valley Road
South Hampton, MA 01703
(800) 355-6813
http://www.ctvalleybio.com

Fisher Science Education
485 South Frontage Road
Burr Ridge, IL 60521
http://www.fisheredu.com

Frey Scientific
P.O. Box 8101
100 Paragon Parkway
Mansfield, OH 44903
(800) 225-3739
http://www.freyscientific.com

Neo/SCI Corporation
P.O. Box 22729
210 Commerce Drive
Rochester, NY 14692-2729
(800) 526-6689
http://www.neosci.com

Urbana Laboratories
(Root nodule bacteria)
P.O. Box 1393
St. Joseph MO, 64502
(816) 223-3446
http://www.urbana-labs.com/

LEARN MORE ABOUT IT

NEAT WEBSITES

About the Human Internet
http://home.about.com
Type in "nature" and join various online guides for explorations, including the best new content, relevant links, how-to's, forums, and answers to just about any question.

Acid Rain
http://www.epa.gov/airmarkets
Learn about acid rain and its impacts.

Amphibian Egg Development
http://www.luc.edu/depts/biology/dev/stages.htm
Observe time-lapse images of developing grassfrog eggs (*Rana pipiens*).

Backyard Habitats
http://www.enature.com
Create backyard bird habitats.

Biodiversity
http://biodiversity.uno.edu
This is a biodiversity and biological collections web server.

Biofilms—The Microbial World
http://helios.bto.ed.ac.uk/bto/microbes/biofilm.htm
Explore biofilms; learn what they are and where they are found. This site contains great links to other microlife forms.

Cornell Composting

http://www.cfe.cornell.edu/compost/Composting_homepage.html
This website is specifically geared to schools, providing information on ideas for student research projects, indoor and outdoor composting projects, compost quizzes, and science and engineering principles.

Database Browser (Gopher)

http://www.cis.ohio-state.edu/htbin/rfc/rfc1580.html
This is a guide to Internet resource tools.

Dendrochronology

http://web.utk.edu/~grissino
The ultimate website for learning about tree rings.

Field Guides

http://www.enature.com
Search the online field guides (insects, butterflies, seashells, and sea creatures), find detailed species descriptions, and then save your own notes.

Fungi Projects

http://www.mycomasters.com/Science-fair-projects.html
This site suggests science fair project ideas using mushrooms and fungi.

Insects

http://netvet.wustl.edu/invert.htm
This is a website link resource to the insects.

Laboratory Safety

http://www.acs.ucalgary.ca/~ucsafety/bulletins/genlab1.htm
This is a resource for general laboratory safety.

Looking at Invertebrates

http://www.umesci.maine.edu/ams/inverts.htm
This is a website link resource to the invertebrates, including museums.

Looking at Plants

http://plants.usda.gov

The PLANTS database is a source of standardized information about plants. This database focuses on vascular plants, mosses, liverworts, hornworts, and lichens of the United States and its territories.

Microbe Zoo

http://www.commtechlab.msu.edu/sites/dlc-me/zoo/index.html

This is a digital learning center for microbiology. Discover the many worlds of hidden microbes in the soil, on food, in other animals, and in the water.

Microlife Tour

http://www.microscopy-uk.org.uk/mag/wimsmall/smal3.html

Take a peek at bacteria, protists, and microcrustaceans that inhabit ponds and other familiar places.

Microscopy Society of America

http://www.microscopy.com

This is an excellent microscopy resource, which includes a virtual microscopy lab and the opportunity to "Ask a Microscopist" questions.

Optics for Kids

http://www.Opticalres.com/kidoptx.htm#startkidoptx

Learn about light, lenses, magnifying glasses, lasers, and more.

Owl Fact Sheet

http://www.conservation.state.mo.us/nathis/birds/owl/owl-fact.html

Learn about owls and how to build owl nest boxes.

Peterson Guide Series

http://petersononline.com

Special features include bird identification, the basics of birdwatching, articles and publications on birds and birdwatching, and terrific links and resources.

Project Feeder Watch
http://birds.cornell.edu/PFW
This is an annual survey of birds that visit feeders each winter.

Science Fair Project Guidelines
http://www.ipl.org/yout/
The Internet Public Library is an invaluable resource for students and parents—offering assistance in math, science, computers, and much more.

Search Engines
http://www.squirrelnet.com
This site offers a listing of the top 20 engines, with search tips.

Whyville
http://www.whyville.com
This is an online community for parents and kids dedicated to learning through exploration and communication.

SOFTWARE
WORD-PROCESSING PROGRAMS

AmiPro
http://www.lotus.com/home.nsf/welcome/products

Microsoft Word
http://www.microsoft.com/office/word/evaluation/guide.htm

WordPro
http://www.lotus.com/home.nsf/welcome/products

SPREADSHEET PROGRAMS
Create, analyze, and share important data quickly.

Excel
http://www.microsoft.com/office/Excel

Lotus 1-2-3
http://www.lotus.com/home.nsf/welcome/products

GRAPHING

Graphical Analysis
http://www.vernier.com/soft/ga.html
Written specifically for science classes, this inexpensive, easy-to-learn program creates a graph as the data are entered. The graphs follow accepted scientific graphing conventions. Graphs can be scaled and the style of the graphs can be changed to best display the data.

DATABASE

FileMaker Pro
http://www.filemaker.com/products/try_filemaker.html
Create lists, data sets, and data-centered reports easily.

BIBLIOGRAPHY

Able, K. *Gathering of Angels: Migrating Birds and Their Ecology.* Cornell University Press, 1999.

The Acid Rain Story. Information Directorate, Environment Canada, Ottawa, Ontario, K1A OH3.

Acid Rain: What It Is—How You Can Help! National Wildlife Federation, 1412 16th Street NW, Washington, DC 20036.

Appelhof, M., and M. Fenton. *Worms Eat My Garbage: How to Set Up and Maintain a Worm Composting System.* Flower Press, 1997.

Ball, L., and J. Anderson. *Composting.* Workman Publishing, 1998.

Biederman, M.A., and F. Barth. *Insects and Flowers: The Biology of a Partnership.* Princeton University Press, 1991.

Blakemore, R.P. "Magnetotactic Bacteria." *Science* 190: 377–9, 1975.

Blakemore, R.P., and R.B. Frankel. "Magnetic Migration and Bacteria." *Scientific American* 245(6): 58–65, 1981.

Bleifeld, M. *Experimenting with a Microscope.* New York: Watts, 1988.

Brady, N.C. *The Nature and Property of Soils.* Prentice Hall, 1999.

The Brine Shrimp and How to Hatch Its Eggs. San Francisco: San Francisco Aquarium Society, California Academy of Sciences, 1978.

Bronmark, C., and L. Hansson. *The Biology of Lakes & Ponds*. Oxford University Press, 1998.

Buchsbaum, R., and J. Peasrse. *Animals Without Backbones*. 3rd ed. University of Chicago Press, 1987.

Bulloch, William. *The History of Bacteriology*. New York: Dover, 1979.

Caduto, M., and J. Thomson. *Pond and Brook: A Guide to Nature in Freshwater Environments*. University Press of New England, 1990.

Camilleri, T., and S. Camilleri. *Carnivorous Plants*. New York: Simon & Schuster, 2000.

Casselman, K. *Craft of the Dyer: Colour from Plants and Lichens*. New York: Dover, 1993.

Cottam, C. *Insects: A Guide to Familiar American Insects*. New York: Golden Press, 1987.

D'Amato, P. *The Savage Garden: Cultivating Carnivorous Plants*. Ten Speed Press, 1998.

De Kruif, Paul. *Microbe Hunters*. San Diego: Harcourt Brace, 1966.

Demrow, C., and D. Saliisbury. *The Complete Guide to Trail Building and Maintenance*. Appalachian Mountain Club, 1998.

Dobell, C. *Antony van Leeuwenhoek and His Little Animals*. New York: Dover, 1969.

Garber, S. *The Urban Naturalist*. New York: Dover, 1998.

Gralla, P., et al. *How the Internet Works*. 5th ed. Que Corp., 1999.

Grave, E. *Using the Microscope: A Guide for Naturalists*. New York: Dover, 1991.

Grenard, S., and W. Love. *Amphibians: Their Care and Keeping*. IDG Books, 1999.

Hale, M.E. *How to Know the Lichens*. 2nd ed. Dubuque, Iowa: William C. Brown, 1979.

Harrington, R. *FilemakerPro*. Windows Academy, 1997.

Headstrom, Richard. *Adventures with Insects*. New York: Dover, 1982.

Hershey, D. *Plant Biology Science Projects*. New York: John Wiley & Sons, 1995.

Hitch, C.J. "Dendrochronology and Serendipity." *American Scientist* 70: 300–305, 1982.

How to Make an Insect Collection. Rochester, N.Y.: Ward's Natural Science Establishment, 1990. No. 32W2196.

Imes, R. *The Practical Entomologist.* Fireside, 1992.

Jahn, Theodore L., et al. *How to Know the Protozoa.* 2nd ed. Dubuque, Iowa: William C. Brown, 1979.

Knutson, R.M. "Plants in Heat." *Natural History* 88: 42–47, 1979.

Krieger, M. *How to Excel in Science Competitions* (Science Fair Success). Enslow, 1999.

Laessoe, T. et al. *Eyewitness Handbooks: Mushrooms.* Dorling Kindersley, 1998.

Lavies, B. *Compost Critters.* E.P. Dutton, 1993.

Lawlor, E. and P. Archer. *Discover Nature in Water & Wetlands: Things to Know and Things to Do.* Stackpole Books, 2000.

Lawrence, Gale. *The Indoor Naturalist: Observing the World of Nature Inside Your Home.* New York: Prentice-Hall, 1986.

Levine, John et al. *The Internet for Dummies.* 7th ed. New York: IDG Books, 2000.

Levine, S. et al. *Fun with Your Microscope.* Sterling Publications, 1998.

Lincoln, R., and G. Boxshall. *The Cambridge Illustrated Dictionary of Natural History.* New York: Cambridge University Press, 1990.

Margulis, L. *Symbiotic Planet: A New Look at Evolution.* New York: Perseus Books, 2000.

Margulis, L. and D. Sagan. *The Microcosmos Coloring Book.* Orlando, Fla: Harcourt Brace, 1988.

—— *Microcosmos: 4 Billion Years of Evolution from Our Microbial Ancestors.* University of California Press, 1997.

Margulis, L., and Karlene Schwartz. *Five Kingdoms: An Illustrated Guide to the Phyla of Life on Earth.* 3rd ed. New York: Freeman, 1998.

Matossian, M.K. "Ergot and the Salem Witchcraft Affair." *American Scientist* 70(4): 355–357, 1982.

Mattison, C. *The Care of Reptiles and Amphibians in Captivity.* New York: Sterling, 1992.

McKnight, K. Edited by V. Peterson. *A Field Guide to Mush-rooms: North America*. Boston: Houghton Mifflin, 1998.

Miller, Orson, Jr. *Mushrooms of North America*. New York: Dutton, 1985.

Milne, Lorus J., and Margery Milne. *The Audubon Society Field Guide to North American Insects and Spiders*. New York: Knopf, 1980.

Mitchell, John. *A Field Guide to Your Own Backyard*. New York: Norton, 1985.

Morgan, S. *Acid Rain*. New York: Watts, 1999.

Needham, J., and P. Needham. *A Guide to the Study of Freshwater Biology*. 5th ed. San Francisco: Holden-Day, 1989.

Morse, D.H. "Milkweeds and Their Visitors." *Scientific American* 253: 112–119, 1985.

Mozart, H. *Guppies: Keeping and Breeding in Captivity*. Chelsea House, 1998.

Neiring, W. *The Audubon Society Field Guide to North American Wildflowers: Eastern Region*. New York: Knopf, 1994.

Nicholls, R. *Beginning Hydroponics: Soilless Gardening*. Running Press, 1990.

Orlans, B. *Animal Care from Protozoa to Small Mammals*. New York: Addison-Wesley, 1977.

Peckarsky, B., et al. *Freshwater Macroinvertebrates of Northeastern North America*. Cornell University Press, 1990.

Pendergrass, W. *Carolina Protozoa and Invertebrates Manual*. Burlington, N.C.: Carolina Biological Supply Co., 1980. No. 45-3904.

Peterson, L. *A Field Guide to Eastern Edible Wild Plants*. Boston: Houghton Mifflin, 1984.

——— *A Field Guide to Trees and Shrubs*. 2nd ed. Boston: Houghton Mifflin, 1993.

Peterson, R. *Birds* Peterson First Guides Series. Boston: Houghton Mifflin, 1986.

——— *A Guide to Animal Tracks*. Boston: Houghton Mifflin, 1998.

Pramer, D., and N. Dondero. "Microscopic Traps." *Natural History* 66(10): 540, 1957.

Rainis, Kenneth G. *Exploring with a Magnifying Glass*. Danbury, Conn.: Venture, 1995.

Rainis, K., and B. Russell. *Guide to Microlife*. Danbury, Conn.: Watts, 1996.

Red Herring: Myths and Facts about Acid Rain. The Izaak Walton League of America, 1800 North Kent Street, Suite 806, Arlington, VA. 22209.

Reid, G.K. *Pond Life: A Guide to Common Plants and Animals of North American Ponds and Lakes*. New York: Golden Press, 1987.

Roberto, K. *How To Hydroponics*. FutureGarden, 2000.

Rogers, K. *Complete Book of the Microscope*. EDC Publications, 1999.

Rolfe, R.T., and F.W. Rolfe. *The Romance of the Fungus World*. New York: Dover, 1974.

Ruppert, E., and R.S. Fox. *Seashore Animals of the Southeast*. Columbia, S.C.: University of South Carolina Press, 1988.

Sagan, Carl. *Cosmos*. New York: Ballantine Books, 1993.

Sagan, Dorion, and Lynn Margulis. *Garden of Microbial Delights: A Practical Guide to the Subvisible World*. New York: Harcourt Brace Jovanovich, 1988.

Snedden R. *The Benefits of Bacteria*. Heinemann Library, 2000.

——— *A World of Microorganisms*. Heinemann Library, 2000.

Spellenberg, R. *The Audubon Society Field Guide to North American Wildflowers: Western Region*. New York: Knopf, 1994

Stokes, D. *A Guide to Nature in Winter*. Boston: Little, Brown, 1979.

——— *A Guide to Observing Insect Lives*. Boston: Little, Brown, 1984.

Stokes, M., and T. Smiley. *An Introduction to Tree-Ring Dating*. University of Arizona Press, 1996.

Tompkins, P., and C. Bird. *The Secret Life of Plants*. New York: HarperCollins, 1989.

Tyson, P. *Acid Rain (Earth at Risk)*. Chelsea House, 1992.

An Updated Perspective on Acid Rain. Edison Electric Institute, 1111 19th Street. NW, Washington, DC, 20036. (Free.)

Vitt, D., et. al *Mosses, Lichens & Ferns of Northwest North America*. Lone Pine Publishers, 1993.

Wolf, A., and M. Hill. *The Art of Photographing Nature*. New York: Crown, 1993.

Whitten, R.H. *Use, Care and Culture of Invertebrates in the Classroom*. Burlington, N.C.: Carolina Biological Supply Company, 1980.

Zappler, G., and L. Zappler. *Amphibians as Pets*. New York: Doubleday, 1973.

Zim, H., and H. Smith. *Reptiles and Amphibians*. New York: Golden Press, 1987.

INDEX